50
ways
to improve
women's
lives

50 ways
to improve
women's
lives

the essential women's guide for
achieving equality, health, and success

National Council of Women's Organizations

Introduction by **Martha Burk**,
Chair of the National Council of Women's Organizations

Inner Ocean Publishing, Inc.
Maui, Hawai'i ✦ San Francisco, California

Inner Ocean Publishing, Inc.
P.O. Box 1239
Makawao, Maui, HI 96768-1239

Cover design by Laura Beers
Book design by Maxine Ressler

PUBLISHER CATALOGING-IN-PUBLICATION DATA
National Council of Women's Organizations
    50 ways to improve women's lives : the essential women's guide for achieving equality, health, and success / National Council of Women's Organizations ; introduction by Martha Burk. – 1st ed. – Maui, Hawaii : Inner Ocean, 2005.
        p. ; cm.
        ISBN: 1-930722-45-1
        1. Women – Social conditions. 2. Women – Health and hygiene. 3. Women's rights. 4. Feminism. 5. Self-realization in women. 6. Women – Psychology. I. Title. II. Fifty ways to improve women's lives.
HQ1233 .F54 2005
305.42 – dc22   0503

Printed in the United States of America on recycled paper

05 06 07 08 09 10   DATA   10 9 8 7 6 5 4 3 2 1

Distributed by Publishers Group West

For information on promotions, bulk purchases, premiums, or educational use, please contact 866.731.2216 or sales@innerocean.com.

To all the leaders and activists, women and men, who work to improve women's lives.

Special thanks to all of our contributors, publisher Karen Bouris, editor Angela Watrous, and NCWO consultant Mal Johnson, who are helping us to reach out to women everywhere.

Contents

Introduction · **Martha Burk,**
   Chair of the National Council of Women's Organizations   1

section 1   Do It for Your Health   5

   Preserve a Healthy Environment · **Jan Schakowsky**   6
   Get Health Care for Everyone · **Dixie Horning**   9
   Protect Reproductive Rights · **Vicki Saporta**   12
   Ensure Sexual Health · **Gloria Feldt**   14
   Treat Your Body Well · **Diana Zuckerman**   17
   Provide Access to Mental Health Care · **Lori Valencia Greene**   20
   Support Healthy Aging · **Laura M. Young**   23

section 2   Practice Real Family Values   27

   Secure Prenatal Care Globally · **Ileana Ros-Lehtinen**   28
   Make Child Care a National Priority · **Helen Blank**   31
   End the Era of Latchkey Children · **Leslie J. Calman**   33
   Guarantee Paid Sick Leave · **Rosa L. De Lauro**   36
   Reform Welfare · **Heidi Hartmann and Cynthia Harrison**   39
   Stop Domestic Violence · **Lorraine Cole**   42
   Uphold Peace in Your Community · **Sarah Harder**   45

section 3   Grow Your Money, Grow Your Mind   47

   Achieve Higher Levels of Education · **Lisa M. Maatz**   48
   Champion Women's Studies · **Ellen Boneparth**   51

Demand Pay Equity · **Nancy L. Hurlbert** 54

Reach Economic Self-Sufficiency · **Joan A. Kuriansky** 57

Consume Wisely · **Cathleen Witter** 60

Promote Financial Literacy · **Stacey Stewart** 63

Advance Women in Business · **Hedy M. Ratner** 65

Prepare for Retirement · **Cindy Hounsell** 68

section 4   Lead the Way 71

Advocate for Women in the Media · **Eleanor Smeal** 72

Get Every Woman to Vote · **Kim Gandy** 75

Nourish Women's Ambitions · **Marie Wilson** 77

Develop Political Leaders · **Karen O'Connor** 79

Run for Office · **Dianne Feinstein** 82

Recognize Women in the Military · **Captain Lory Manning** 84

Equalize Constitutional Rights · **Carolyn B. Maloney** 87

Reassess National Priorities · **Susan Shaer** 90

section 5   Forge a Path for the Next Generation 93

Mentor Women and Girls · **Alison Stein** 94

Teach Honest Sex Education · **Martha E. Kempner** 97

Liberate Girls from Abuse · **Jill J. Morris** 100

Support Girls and Women in Sports · **Donna A. Lopiano** 103

Celebrate Women's Achievements · **Molly Murphy MacGregor** 106

Gain Daily Access to Science and Technology
Shireen Mitchell 109

Engage in a New Wave of Activism · **Mia Herndon** 112

section 6   Build the Community You Want to Live In   115

Create Community Media · **Frieda Werden**   116

Put a Stop to Sexual Harassment · **Marty Langelan**   119

Eradicate Racism · **Mal Johnson and C. DeLores Tucker**   122

Insist on Equal Rights for Lesbians · **Patricia Ireland**   125

Value Diversity and Promote Cultural Understanding
  Kiran Ahuja   128

Mandate Responsible Gun Policy · **Mary Leigh Blek**   131

Support Labor Unions · **Pamela Wilson**   134

section 7   Reach for the World   137

Uphold Women's Rights as Human Rights · **Sarah C. Albert**   138

Address the Unique Needs of Immigrant Women
  Hilda L. Solis   141

Combat Human Trafficking · **Melanne Verveer**   144

Wage Peace around the World · **Swanee Hunt**   147

Impact Foreign Policy · **June Zeitlin**   150

Invest in Women Internationally · **Elaine Zuckerman**   152

Afterword: Women at the Global Decision-Making Table
  Madeleine K. Albright   155

Endnotes   157

Resources   168

Contributors   175

Introduction

You've taken the first step: you have picked up this book. We hope it will be the first of many steps on your path to enacting change for women – in your personal life, in your community, and in the world at large.

The book is brought to you by the National Council of Women's Organizations (NCWO), the nation's largest and oldest coalition of women's groups with over 200 organizations collectively representing ten million women. We work on all aspects of progress for women – from equal pay, domestic violence, and child care to reproductive rights, political leadership, and global equality. Our groups are diverse: some have thousands of members; some produce research; some defend women's rights through legal means; some offer direct services to women. We work on different issues, yet we all have one desire: to see progress for women. We know you share that goal, and we hope this book can provide a blueprint to invigorate your interest, commitment, and creativity.

As chair of the NCWO, in May of 2004, I was asked by the All-China Women's Federation to come to China and deliver a speech to their members. My topic was "The State of Women in the United States." Easy enough, I thought, until I sat down to write and realized that there were many ways I could approach the subject. I could discuss how women in this country are doing in comparison to women in China or to women worldwide. Or I could talk about how American women compare to American men – socially, economically, and politically. Still another approach would be to compare American women today to American women at the turn of the 20th century, before we even had the vote. Or I could focus on the current state of U.S. women compared to an ideal – where we would be if we could indeed "have it all."

Depending on the angle I chose, I could make a compelling and valid case that we're doing very well, pretty well, or not so good. We're either headed in the right direction or we're losing ground. From my perspective as a leader in the women's movement, I've come to believe that it's important to view the issues from all vantage points: we must look at the losses we've suffered alongside the enormous gains we made in the 1960s and 1970s. Yes, we've achieved parity with men in obtaining college degrees, but politicians have recently tried to weaken the law guaranteeing equal educational opportunities for girls. While we have achieved equal access to credit, as well as pregnancy leave and the right to seek any job, we're still lagging behind men in how much we're paid, and that gap is widening. Our right to control our reproductive lives, a hard-fought battle won in the Supreme Court in 1973, is now one judicial appointment away from being overturned. Our standard of living is high, but adult women still comprise the majority of minimum-wage workers. And finally, we have universal health care for retirees, but elderly women are the largest group living in poverty.

I stressed in this speech that we must all play an active role in protecting the progress we've made and that we must work hard to improve the lives of women even more. When my address ended, one of the American delegates came up to me and made a simple but profound request: "Just tell me ten things that I personally can do to make change," she said. And with that, I saw that there was a great need for a book such as this. A book that could speak to women who weren't policy experts or traveling to conventions in China but who were *living* the issues that we speak so passionately about. And instead of 10 ideas, we're suggesting 50 to give you something to chew on.

We have gathered 50 leading experts to describe the issues and to offer concrete, doable things to help, no matter how much or little time you have to dedicate to these causes at any given moment. We've taken a varied approach on the issues that most impact the quality of your and other women's lives. Some essays, such as "Treat Your Body Well" and "Make Child Care a National Priority," examine the personal concerns that affect our daily lives. Other essays, such as "Wage Peace around the World" and Madeleine Albright's afterword "Women at the Global Decision-Making Table" look at women's lives through a global lens. Still others, such as "Demand Pay Equity" and "Nourish Women's Ambitions," point to specific areas where American women are not being afforded the same opportunities as American men. In the essay "Equalize Constitutional

Rights,"we learn how the work started by our foremothers still needs our attention. And last but certainly not least, in essays like "Celebrate Women's Achievements," we learn how to support the ideals that will inspire us to keep moving forward, even when the odds seem stacked against positive change.

We've grouped the essays into sections to illustrate the particular inter-connections among certain issues. We start with the section "Do It for Your Health," because without good health for ourselves, our loved ones, and our planet, we can't accomplish much in other areas. Section 2, "Prac-tice Real Family Values," lays out how to achieve safety and security for our homes and our communities. In section 3, "Grow Your Money, Grow Your Mind," the essayists recommend ways to strengthen women's edu-cational opportunities and economic security. While the idea that women "belong" in a political body is no longer novel, neither has "belonging" been entirely realized – so section 4, "Lead the Way," shows us how to sup-port women in the realms of media, politics, the military, and other fields that redefine national priorities. Because our girls are the hope for future progress, section 5, "Forge a Path for the Next Generation," discusses a variety of ways in which older women can act as mentors and younger women can make new paths to progress. In section 6, "Build the Com-munity You Want to Live In," the authors speak frankly about the walls that divide us, and how we can break down prejudices and work together. And finally, section 7, "Reach for the World," examines how U.S. women can help protect the human rights of women worldwide.

When reading about the 50 issues covered in these pages and making your own plan of action, ask yourself: As American women, are we doing very well, pretty well, or not so good? Are we headed in the right direction, or are we losing ground? I suspect you'll find that the answer is not sim-ple and the solutions are not necessarily easy. But almost every woman can do something. 50 *Ways to Improve Women's Lives* is not meant to be read at one sitting. Reading over the book and starting small can give you a taste of how good it feels to be a part of the solution to the problems impacting the women in your community, your country, and your world.

Now we'd like to suggest that you take another step. Find five to ten women you are connected with and start your own grassroots women's civic action group. Women have been getting together since time immemorial, from gathering at quilting guilds to forming book clubs to organizing girls' nights out. We want to encourage you to turn your passion, daring, and love of community into action, and we're providing you all the tools to do so at our website, www.womensorganizations.org. After coming together, review the 50 ways to improve women's lives that we offer in this book, and choose one of the essays that resonates most with *your* group. What do you feel most compelled to act on? Is it guaranteeing better child care, seeing a woman president someday (soon), or supporting women in sports? What kind of world do you want your children to grow up in, and what do you feel must change? What personal experiences have you had that determine where your courage lies and how you can engage?

NCWO has a motto: "One woman can change the world – but it's easier when you work in groups." Discover what works best for your group, meet monthly, and, together, we can change the world. Think about how much we have already done.

Martha Burk

Do It for Your Health

Preserve a Healthy Environment

Jan Schakowsky, U.S. Representative

I f you've ever inhaled the fumes of a passing bus or a nearby factory or been unable to drink water straight from your own sink, you understand how much environmental issues affect your daily life. Yet the impact of pollution on the body lasts beyond a momentary gasp for fresh air or a bad-tasting sip of water. In 1970, Congress passed the Clean Air Act to protect the public from the known risks of air pollution, such as increased rates of asthma and premature death from lung cancer and heart disease. Yet 30 years later, more than half of the American population – approximately 160 million people – are still breathing unhealthy air.[1]

The toll of air pollution on a woman's body is particularly high. Environmental factors have a major impact on women's general and reproductive health; they contribute to cancer, respiratory problems, and autoimmune diseases, to name a few consequences. And for those of us who become pregnant, all the toxins in our bodies are directly transferred to our developing fetuses.

Numerous pollutants in our water and air supplies bombard our bodies every day. Mercury, for example, is a particularly toxic pollutant that causes brain damage and interferes with the development of fetuses, babies, and small children. One child in six born in the United States could be at risk for developmental disorders because of mercury exposure in their mothers' wombs – that adds up to 630,000 children each year.[2]

Power plants, the primary uncontrolled source of mercury pollution, contribute about 48 tons of mercury to our air every year. Once mercury is released into the air, it settles into our lakes, streams, and rivers. To date, federal, state, and local officials have found mercury pollution in 12 million acres of lakes, estuaries, and wetlands – 30 percent of the national total – and 473,000 miles of streams, rivers, and coastlines. After mercury enters our water, it travels up the food chain, contaminating tuna, lobster, halibut, sea bass, trout, and crab, among other marine life. It's estimated that as many as 60,000 babies born each year in the United States suffer from neurological damage caused by their mothers' consumption of mercury-contaminated fish.[3]

In 2000, the U.S. Environmental Protection Agency (EPA) recognized the huge threat that mercury poses to women and to the general public health. The EPA ruled that power plants must use the best available technology to remove that hazardous substance from our environment. Under the EPA's 2000 ruling, power plants would have reduced their mercury emissions 90 percent by 2008.

Under new leadership, however, the EPA reversed its position in 2004, proposing new power-plant regulations that would require only a 50 to 70 percent reduction by 2018. The EPA's new proposal essentially ignored the agency's own expert analysis and disregarded the recommendations of the panel of stakeholders that the agency appointed to work on this issue. Instead, the new proposal catered to the powerful energy industry lobby, placing a higher value on the industry's profits than on the health of women, children, and our communities.

Environmentalists and public health advocates worked with outraged public officials, including myself, to get citizens to speak out against the proposed regulations. The public outcry succeeded in delaying the final regulations and in convincing the EPA to commit to doing additional analysis on the issue before making any final decisions, extending the deadline for the final rule to March 15, 2005.

We have a right to clean air and water, to good health for ourselves and our families. Our challenge is to fight for strong regulations, force the EPA to enforce these regulations, and require the energy industry to adhere to meaningful and rapid reductions in mercury pollution. We owe it to ourselves and to future generations – for the health and well-being of us all.

> ≥ **CALL TO ACTION** ≤

+ Learn more about environmental health and its relation to women's lives (www.niehs.nih.gov/external/facts.htm).

- Contact one of the many organizations committed to environmental health and justice (see Resources).

- Go to the EPA's website and register your opinions and comments at http://docket.epa.gov/edkpub/index.jsp.

- Learn where candidates stand on environmental issues. The League of Conservation Voters (www.lcv.org) provides a scorecard on how your elected officials voted on environmental issues.

- Make your views known when environmental legislation or regulations are being considered.

- Commit to meaningful action in your daily life by recycling, using energy-efficient transportation and power, consuming wisely, and preserving a healthy environment.

Get Health Care for Everyone

Dixie Horning, Executive Director,
UCSF National Center of Excellence in Women's Health

Several years ago, I gathered with a group of friends. My dear friend Yolanda, a 35-year-old Latina, was upset that night, having just lost her mother on the heels of giving birth to her second child. Bereft, she went off to lie down and have some private moments of reflection.

A few minutes later, I went to check on her and was shocked to find her in a cold sweat. She complained of feeling dizzy and having pain in her neck and jaw. Even though she wasn't experiencing chest pain, it seemed like a heart attack: I called 911 and rushed back to our friends, some of whom were doctors and nurses. Everyone denied the possibility that Yolanda could be having a heart attack. "She's too young," they said, as well as, "Hispanic women don't have heart conditions" and, "It must be stress or a panic attack." But I couldn't let go of my fears. When the EMTs arrived, they too said it wasn't possible for her to be having a heart attack. After she arrived at the hospital and went through several inconclusive tests, the doctors performed an EKG. Later that night, Yolanda had a quadruple bypass. She almost died, due to an incorrect assumption that a woman of her age and ethnic background couldn't have heart disease. As this story illustrates, the medical community still knows little about the health of women, particularly women of color, largely because the vast majority of health studies and medication trials have been done on white men alone. Put another way, if more health studies and medication trials included diverse groups of women, then doctors, nurses, and consumers would know a lot more about women's health.

Perhaps even more distressing is the fact that if Yolanda hadn't so recently given birth, she would not have had medical coverage that night. Without insurance, she might have received less aggressive care or no care at all.

Uninsured or underinsured women are at higher risk for disease, chronic illness, unintended pregnancy, and other negative conditions, and women with insurance typically have better health outcomes than uninsured women.[4] However, over 15 percent of women under age 65[5] still lack access to basic health care services, including preventive and prenatal care. The number of uninsured women in the United States has grown faster than the number of men, specifically three times faster,[6] and women of color are more likely to be uninsured than white women.[7]

Women of all ethnic, racial, and socioeconomic groups continue to experience inequities and neglect in health care. So do their families. It is a tragedy when a family must be selective about who gets care. Our country's policies are literally making families choose who will live, who will die, and who will suffer with chronic pain. We deserve better health care.

To improve the health and quality of life for women and their families, our country must adopt a cohesive and dynamic approach to these problems by enacting universal health care coverage. Found in all other industrialized countries, universal health care would ensure affordable coverage for all. Also known as a single-payer system, it is endorsed by many national organizations.[8] Some people fear that it will require an increase in income taxes, that it veers to close to socialism, or that the decline of quality medical care will follow. In reality, the United States already spends more for health care than any other country; yet the money is not being distributed proportionately, and many possible financing schemes (besides raising taxes) do exist.[9] Support for universal health care is growing. In March 2004, 125 cities observed Health Care Action Day to promote comprehensive health care reform. Other events happen throughout the year, so that everyone may learn about the possibilities of universal health care and get involved.

+ Consider how lack of access to high-quality, timely, continuous preventative care affects your health. Are you uninsured, or do you know people who are uninsured?

+ Learn more about universal health care at www.grahamazon.com/sp/index.php.

+ Sign up with Americans for Health Care at www.americansforhealth care.com/index.cfm.

+ Get involved with organizations like UHCAN: Universal Health Care Action Network (www.uhcan.org).

+ Vote for candidates who support universal health care.

+ Write letters to your representatives in Congress and tell them to support single-payer health care.

+ Find out what actions are going on in your state and get involved.

Protect Reproductive Rights

Vicki Saporta, President and CEO, National Abortion Federation

Despite the fact that one out of three women of reproductive age in America will have had an abortion by the age of 45,[10] we live in a time where state and federal legislative attacks on abortion and reproductive rights have reached unprecedented levels. Anti-choice extremists also continue to threaten abortion providers and their clinics with acts of violence. Since 1977, the National Abortion Federation has documented more than 4,200 incidents of clinic violence against abortion providers.[11] To counter this, women are speaking out about their abortion experiences, and abortion providers are furnishing accurate medical information and speaking out against clinic violence in the effort to protect reproductive rights.

In January 1998, Emily Lyons's life changed forever after an anti-choice extremist bombed the abortion clinic where she worked as a nurse. The bombing left one police officer dead and Emily severely injured. Although the crippling experience took away her ability to drive and work, it did not take away her ability to speak out against clinic violence. In July 1998, Representative Henry Hyde was leading efforts to amend the law and protect anti-choice extremists from being prosecuted for criminal conspiracy. Emily testified to help defeat this anti-choice legislative attempt. "In the last six and a half months, I've spent almost 30 hours on the operating table in nine different operations, only to still have dozens of pieces of shrapnel left permanently in my body," Lyons testified. "I am not interested in sympathy. However, I am determined to make sure that people see the end result of this type of terrorism." Emily's testimony was so effective that the law remained intact.

In 1996, representatives in Congress passed a federal ban on abortion. We at the National Abortion Federation brought forward a group of women who needed abortions after finding out during their wanted pregnancies that they were carrying fetuses with lethal anomalies. These courageous women spoke passionately in congressional briefings and testimonies and to the media about the choice they made to have an abortion in order to protect their health. As one woman said, "We are all here for the women that follow us ... because all women deserve the finest medical care that exists and we want that for them." Moved by their stories, President Clinton invited these women and their families to the White House and told them that it was their stories that convinced him to veto the bill. "This country is deeply indebted to them for being able to speak out," Clinton praised. "We need more families like these."

These two stories help to demonstrate how our individual voices, especially when we work together, really do make a difference. The reproductive rights movement grows stronger with every story shared and every choice affirmed. Although the majority of Americans are pro-choice,[12] we continue to be barraged with anti-choice legislation and actions. This means we must all continue to speak out to protect and advocate for reproductive rights. We need your help to ensure that abortion remains a safe, legal, and accessible reproductive option for all women.

⋛ CALL TO ACTION ⋚

+ Stay informed. Sign up for NAF's Action for Choice Team (ACT) Alerts at www.prochoice.org.

+ Speak out. Tell your personal story to those you know when the issue comes up in conversation. When specific legislation is being considered, contact your elected state and federal representatives, write an editorial for your local paper, or organize a pro-choice rally to publicly voice your support for comprehensive reproductive rights.

+ Join pro-choice organizations such as the National Abortion Federation (www.prochoice.org) to support the providers who make reproductive choice a reality and who ensure that women receive quality care.

+ Support your local reproductive health care providers by volunteering or fundraising. Call your local clinic to see if they need clinic escorts or other help.

Ensure Sexual Health

Gloria Feldt, President, Planned Parenthood Federation of America

Rachel, a teenaged Planned Parenthood client, told us, "My parents are not supportive or even very willing to discuss sex or reproductive health with me.... The clinic has helped me with many things: birth control [I can afford] ... and many kind and informative words. Without them, I do not know what my life would be like now."[13]

Sexual health isn't as simple as making a visit to the gynecologist every year or using contraception every time. It also has a mental health and emotional component. Women – especially young women – are often made to feel ashamed, disempowered, or objectified around expressions of their sexuality. Only when we as a society are honest and open about sexuality and when we recognize that the joyous expression of one's own sexuality is central to being fully human can we truly begin to make responsible choices.

There are still many women for whom access to sexual health care is a rarity. Jenna McKean, co-organizer for the Smith College Student Coalition for the March for Women's Lives, explained why she so passionately fights for reproductive rights: "I grew up on welfare in the ghetto of South Philadelphia. For the women [where] I come from ... choice is basically a myth.... If you are too young, too poor, or a color other than white, then the coat hanger desperation everyone else left behind in the '70s is alive and well for you."[14]

The first step toward ensuring sexual health for all women is making reproductive health care and family planning accessible. We must make family planning services, contraception (including over-the-counter emergency contraception), and reproductive health care available to all women. This also means opposing mandatory parental notification/consent laws, which drive some young people to desperate measures.

The second step is making reproductive health care affordable. Family planning provides the tools women need to reduce the risk of unin-

14   50 WAYS TO IMPROVE WOMEN'S LIVES

tended pregnancy and sexually transmitted infections. The Bush administration's freeze on funding for Title X – which provides uninsured women with access to family planning services, regardless of their ability to pay – is a dangerous step in the wrong direction.

Finally, we must provide women and girls – as well as men of all ages – with comprehensive, medically accurate sexuality education. Abstinence-only (or, more accurately, ignorance-only) sex education is taught in 58 percent of public schools. Since 1996, the federal government has increased funding for these ineffective, dangerous programs by more than 3,000 percent[15] – and has slated $168 million for 2005. We must instead use our resources to teach our nation's girls and women about human growth and development, to help them develop their own decision-making skills, and to provide them with the resources to protect themselves against unintended pregnancy and sexually transmitted infections.

Every woman deserves to be sexually healthy and deserves access to the services that make sexual and reproductive rights meaningful. And since the preponderance of Americans agree that women must have the legal right to make their own reproductive choices,[16] it's time to act like the majority we are. We must immediately address this situation, from the top down and the ground up.

⋝ CALL TO ACTION ⋜

+ Find out if the teachers in your school district teach medically accurate sex education, and if they don't, go to the school board and your legislators and insist they do.

+ Write or email newspapers, magazines, and television programs when they misrepresent reproductive health and rights issues, and praise them when they get it right.

+ Find out where candidates stand on these issues. Then write, email, and call your legislators — at all levels of government — and let them know how important it is to support family planning funding, real sex ed, and other pro-choice positions.

+ Support Planned Parenthood (www.plannedparenthood.org) — and other pro-choice, pro-sex education and women's health organizations — with your money and your voice, and pro-choice politicians with your vote, and tell your friends to do the same (see Resources).

+ Share your own stories and views with younger women, as well as peers. Starting the conversation will encourage them to help spread the word.

Treat Your Body Well

....

Diana Zuckerman, President,
National Research Center for Women & Families

How many women do you know who like the way they look? Are
you one of them?

Like most women, I am well aware of the things I wish I could change
about my physical appearance. But for millions of women, every extra
pound, every new wrinkle, and every deviation from the Barbie body ideal
has become a battleground. Many of us are fighting these battles with fad
diets, eating disorders, ineffective "natural supplements," and plastic surgery or cosmetic injections.

At the same time that so many women are resorting to questionable
quick fixes, too many of us are neglecting our health. Obesity is a national
epidemic, contributing to dramatic increases in serious diseases such as
diabetes, heart disease, osteoarthritis, and even breast cancer. But yo-yo diet-
ing, eating disorders, or expensive and sometimes risky cosmetic procedures are not going to make us healthier and may cause real harm.

Experts estimate that five to ten million Americans suffer from eating
disorders such as anorexia, bulimia, and binge eating – almost all of them
women.[17] Millions gain weight because going on and off impossible diets
usually causes us to add pounds, not lose them. And millions more use
prescription diet pills, not realizing that research shows that these pills
have only a modest impact on weight loss and have side effects that can
cause permanent damage or even death.[18]

So-called natural supplements are a popular strategy to look or feel better, but makers don't have to prove their products are safe or effective
before selling them. This lack of regulation can result in false claims or
dangerous side effects. For example, the weight-loss supplement Ephedra
was banned in 2004 after more than 150 people died,[19] and the makers
of Bloussant, a widely advertised "breast enhancement" product, were

successfully sued by the Federal Trade Commission for making false claims that the product increased breast size.[20]

Last year, more than seven million women (almost a quarter million of them ages 18 and younger) turned to cosmetic surgery and injections of questionable substances in an effort to change the way they look.[21] But these procedures, especially those involving permanent implants, can lead to serious complications, resulting in chronic pain and health problems and the need for additional surgery. Unfortunately, the Food and Drug Administration does not require long-term safety studies before approving any medical products, not even implants. When will we stop risking our lives and our health and instead appreciate ourselves in our gloriously unique imperfections?

⋝ CALL TO ACTION ⋜

+ Urge your Congressional representatives to demand the FDA do more to keep risky products off the market. Ask them to make sure drugs and implants designed for long-term use are tested to make sure they are actually safe for long-term use.

+ Report questionable ads for natural supplements (such as those that claim to enlarge or reduce the size of particular body parts) to the Federal Trade Commission (www.ftc.gov) and check the FTC's list of risky natural supplements.

+ Check the label of any prescription medical product you are considering, especially those that make promises that are vague ("it will change your life!") or unrealistic ("lose weight while eating as much as you want!"). Don't buy medical products online — to be safe, only a doctor who examines you should prescribe your medication, and companies you're not familiar with might be selling contaminated products (see the FDA's advice at www.fda.gov/oc/buyonline/default.htm).

+ Research the risks of medical products on the Internet, and don't let clever ads fool you. "Bestselling" doesn't mean best, or safest. Find

---

out what is really in that pill; for example, the drug Serafem (pre-scribed for menstrual mood disorder) is just a pink-colored version of Prozac (an antidepressant).

+ Contact TV stations to complain about programs that glamorize plas-tic surgery. Call the companies that advertise during those programs and let them know what you think.

+ If you want to lose weight, work off more calories than you consume. You'll be amazed at the difference if you walk more, don't eat while watching TV, and drink fewer sugary fruit drinks and sodas.

+ Regularly give genuine compliments to friends and loved ones about their appearance.

+ Never put yourself down; focus on what you like about yourself and your body.

Provide Access
to Mental Health Care

Lori Valencia Greene, Senior Legislative and Federal Affairs Officer,
American Psychological Association

Mental health problems touch all of our lives in some way. Approximately one in five women will experience an episode of major depression during their lifetimes, and women are at least twice as likely as men to experience a major depressive episode. This means that someone in your life – perhaps your friend, your daughter, or even yourself – is likely to struggle with serious depression at some point.

Depression brings significant personal costs, including poor self-care, increased physical illness, and, at worst, the tragedy of suicide. Major depression can dramatically affect our ability to connect with others and function in society. It can result in disability and job loss, leading to a drop in income and often a significant economic burden. And depressed people are not the only ones who suffer. Having a depressed parent not only increases children's risk for developing depressive and anxiety disorders, but it also impairs their overall functioning and physical health.

Several factors increase an individual's risk for depression and other mental disorders. For instance, serious adverse life events, such as being abused as a child or experiencing any other form of violence, are clearly implicated in the onset of depression.[22] Low-income adults are twice as likely to experience new episodes of major depression.[23] And while women of color experience rates of depression comparable to white women, they are at greater risk of having their depression go unrecognized and untreated.[24]

There are effective treatments for depression and for most other mental health conditions. Unfortunately, many women never receive treatment. It has been well established that women use mental health services more than men. However, the number of women coming for care still represents only a portion of those women who are depressed.[25]

The ongoing social stigma against mental illness keeps many from admitting to their feelings or seeking help. This stigma also allows managed health plans, employers, and government legislation to discriminate against those with mental disorders.

In addition to our society's general lack of knowledge or understanding about mental health care, financial constraints serve as a significant barrier to women receiving treatment. Even if women can access affordable mental health care, which is no small task, lack of child care and transportation can prove overwhelming. Overcoming these odds proves particularly difficult for people suffering from depression, who often already feel hopeless and powerless because of the disorder itself.

By advocating for mental health care and awareness in our personal lives and in our society, we can indeed improve the lives of millions of women and their families. The treatment for these life-impairing disorders is better than ever, and improving all the time. We have the tools. We just need to put them to use.

⋛ CALL TO ACTION ⋐

+ Call your elected representatives and ask them to do the following:

  ❖ Pass mental health parity legislation, including Medicare, which would expand on an existing law by prohibiting group health plans from imposing treatment limitations or financial requirements involving deductibles, copayments and out-of-pocket contributions on mental health benefits unless comparable limitations are applied to medical and surgical benefits.

  ❖ Pass legislation mandating strong legal accountability in managed care reform to ensure that patients receive quality care, including mental health, and that managed health plans are held accountable for their actions.

- Fund the National Institutes of Health's research on women's mental health. In particular, ask for more research for subpopulations of women, including women of color, lesbians, adolescent girls, pregnant and postpartum women, and older women.

- Increase funding for critically needed mental health and substance abuse services, including the Substance Abuse and Mental Health Services Administration.

- Increase access to mental health services for military service members, veterans, and their families, as well as victims of war and terrorism.

- After you speak to your representatives, write a letter to the editor entreating readers to do the same.

- If you know someone who needs mental health services, help them to access resources and care providers (see Resources).

Support Healthy Aging

Laura M. Young, Executive Director, OWL,
The Voice of Midlife and Older Women

For those of you who were hoping to find a step-by-step guide to living well into your 90s in this essay, I am sorry to disappoint you, but like Ponce de León, I am still looking for my own personal fountain of youth. What I can offer is a rough blueprint of changes to the health care system that can help us all live longer, healthier lives.

The first step is continual, quality health care for everyone. In 2004, 45 million Americans did not have health insurance. While older Americans do not represent a significant percentage of this number, today's midlife Americans are tomorrow's older Americans. In 2003, people ages 55 to 64 were more likely than children to lack health insurance entirely (12.9 percent versus 11.6 percent). Fifteen percent of women ages 60 to 64, one in seven, had no health insurance.[26] During midlife, the chronic conditions that will affect people for the rest of their lives start to show up, and without proper treatment these conditions will worsen. We actually need to switch from considering treatment cost containment to considering preventative care above cost.

Our current health care system, based on employment, allows millions of people to fall through the cracks. Working people are increasingly losing health insurance coverage or are unable to afford the coverage offered by their employers. In 2002, almost three-quarters of the adults who were uninsured were working people, and more than half worked full time.[27] In recent years, health care costs have continued to spiral out of control — the average monthly contribution required of employees for health insurance premiums rose about 75 percent between 1993 and 2003, while the median family income increased by only 41 percent during that time.[28] Women, who are more likely to take time out of the workforce for caregiving and more likely to work in low-wage jobs that do not offer health insurance, feel the failures of employment-based insurance more acutely than men.

Although Medicare is a wonderful program that has provided quality health care for older Americans over the past four decades, there are many health care expenses that Medicare does not cover. Because women live longer and are more likely to live in poverty than men, they are more likely to fall through the cracks of the "three-layered" health insurance system for seniors. While Medicare insures nearly everyone age 65 and over, women age 65 and over are less likely than their male counterparts to augment their Medicare coverage with private insurance. In fact, the average woman over 65 who lives alone spends more of her after-tax income on health care than on food.[29]

Another major piece of healthy aging is mental health, which is commonly forgotten about in older Americans. One in five older Americans have a diagnosable mental illness, but less than one-quarter of them get any type of mental health attention, let alone appropriate treatment.[30] Despite popular misconception, mental illness, dementia, and substance abuse are not a normal part of aging, and there is no reason that older adults cannot continue to grow, thrive, and enjoy life. The sooner people get help, the better the long-term outcome and their quality of late life. Undiagnosed and untreated mental illness impacts women in particular, since we are more than twice as likely as men to be diagnosed with depression and because we typically live six years longer, further expanding the opportunity for undiagnosed illness.[31] Currently, when an older person goes to a doctor for treatment of a physical health problem, Medicare pays 80 percent of the bill. For a mental health problem, Medicare pays only 50 percent of the bill. Medicare also does not reimburse doctors for screening for mental illnesses. All of these facts add up to less than enough support to help seniors age comfortably, with the best physical and mental health care possible.

+ Get the facts about older women and health care. Visit www.owl-national.org, and check out the 2004 OWL Mother's Day Report.

+ Prevent osteoporosis by eating a balanced diet rich in calcium and vitamin D and participating in weight-bearing exercise. Get more information on prevention at www.center4policy.org/osteo4-03.html.

+ Don't smoke. For information about quitting, and about how women are targeted by tobacco companies, go to www.center4policy.org/ibrief-05-04smoking.html.

+ Join thousands of supporters in calling for mental health parity in Medicare during the last week of May, Older Americans' Mental Health Week. Check out www.owl-national.org for events in your area.

Practice Real Family Values

Secure Prenatal Care Globally

Ileana Ros-Lehtinen, U.S. Representative

Throughout the world, cultural traditions encourage motherhood, yet ill-equipped health care systems often endanger the health of mothers and their infants. It is crucial that we work to protect the health of pregnant women everywhere. One way we can do this is to help secure accessible and comprehensive prenatal care for women and communities worldwide.

The U.S. Congress has, over the years, worked to create an awareness about the services necessary for a healthy pregnancy. We have made progress here in the United States, where the infant mortality rate (which measures how many children die before their first birthday) stands at 7 babies per 1,000, according to the Centers for Disease Control. But in developing countries, the infant mortality rate is far higher – for example, 156 infants per 1,000 in Niger, 81 per 1,000 in the Congo, 83 per 1,000 in Pakistan, and 67 per 1,000 in India (see www.unicef.org).

While our job in the United States won't be done until all American residents have access to comprehensive prenatal care, we must simultaneously support women in countries where deficient resources prevent them from getting the prenatal care they need. It has been one of my priorities while serving in the U.S. House of Representatives to support financial assistance for developing countries so that they can establish women's health resources and afford birth-related care.

One of the more common and treatable prenatal problems women face in developing countries is obstetric fistula, which occurs when labor is prolonged and complicated. The constant pressure of the baby's head in the birth canal causes a hole, or fistula, to form in or near the vagina, which can cause lifelong incontinence unless the fistula is repaired. While obstetric fistula was eradicated in the United States by the 20th century, it remains a problem in nations that lack the hospitals and practitioners necessary for its elimination.

While obstetric fistula was eradicated in the United States by the 20th century, it remains a problem in nations lacking the hospitals and practitioners needed for its elimination. Minimal access to safe maternity care and to Caesarean sections in developing countries leads to high rates of obstetric fistula. Those most susceptible to its dangers are young girls, pregnant before their bodies are fully developed. After experiencing the effects of fistula, these girls are often shunned from society and abandoned by their families. Unaware of treatment or unable to access it, the victims of this ailment are forced to manage its burdens alone.

According to international estimates, two million girls and women are living with this condition. An estimated 50,000 to 100,000 women sustain an obstetric fistula each year. In developing countries, women needing prenatal care or treatment for fistula often must walk upward of three days to reach a medical facility. Even then, many remain untreated, as the necessary surgery to correct the damage is not available or it's deemed a luxury because women can survive without it.

Obstetric fistula and many other prenatal complications are treatable and preventable afflictions, and only together can we ensure that they're completely eradicated in the rest of the world. I have joined in the efforts to diminish the frequency of obstetric fistula by cosponsoring the Obstetric Fistula Surgical Repair, Assistance, and Prevention Act of 2004 (H.R. 4848). Currently under review in the Committee on International Relations, this bill calls for the establishment of at least 12 treatment centers in countries with high rates of obstetric fistula, with a particular emphasis on nations in Africa.

As the proud mother of two beautiful daughters, I have a sincere passion for the well-being of young women around the world. Women make an indispensable contribution to the growth of world culture. Without our contributions, society is less alive, culture is impoverished, and peace less stable.

+ Support worldwide campaigns and organizations devoted to combating obstetric fistula and its resulting social stigma (see www.end fistula.org, www.engenderhealth.org, and www.fistulahospital.org).

+ Contact your representative to ask that he or she support legislation to expand access to prenatal care, in particular H.R. 4848, to provide funding for fistula treatment.

+ Inform yourself regarding prenatal care in this country. See www.cdc. gov/nchs/fastats/prenatal.htm.

Make Child Care
a National Priority

Helen Blank, Director of Leadership and Public Policy,
National Women's Law Center

O ver the past 50 years, it has become commonplace for women to work outside the home. Nearly two-thirds of women with children under age six and over three-quarters of women with school-aged children are in the labor force.[1] Not only are there few possibilities for paid leave from work after the birth of a child, but there's also a dearth of infant care options.

Just finding child care is a challenge, but finding high-quality child care is even more difficult. Only ten states require child care centers to have child/staff ratios that meet the recommendations of early childhood educators.[2] Thirty states allow teachers in child care centers to begin working with children before receiving any training in child development.[3]

For women at all income levels, the costs of child care can be staggering. It can easily cost $4,000 to $10,000 a year – more than the average cost of public college tuition.[4] And unlike college costs, families often face these child care expenses when they are just beginning their careers and when they have not yet been able to build up savings.

Over the past two decades, we have made some progress enacting policies to help families with child care costs, but it has been limited and still leaves millions of women and their children behind. Stagnant federal funding since 2001, combined with state budget gaps, has resulted in less help for families and reduced support for already overburdened child care providers.[5]

The federal child care tax credit – which was expanded in 2001 for the first time in 20 years – reimburses families for a portion of their child care expenses. However, because this credit is not refundable, it rarely helps the families who need it most: low-income families with no income tax liability. Twenty-seven states (including the District of Columbia) have their own child care tax credits, but only 13 states offer refundable credits.[6]

Child care assistance can make a real difference in women's lives. It enables some to go back to school, earn a degree, and get a job with better pay. Reliable child care allows others the peace of mind they need to concentrate at work. For many, it can reduce the stress that comes from piecing together child care arrangements that can easily fall through. High-quality child care is also essential to children's successful development. Supporting access to quality child care for all families positively impacts our daily lives and our children's futures.

≥ CALL TO ACTION ≤

+ Take full advantage of available help with child care costs: subsidies (if you are eligible), the federal child care tax credit and any state credits, and (if your employer offers one) a flexible savings account for child care expenses. Go to www.nwlc.org for more information.

+ Find out if your state has a refundable tax credit at www.nwlc.org. If it does, take advantage of the credit; if it doesn't, NWLC has suggestions for how to advocate for that tax credit.

+ Encourage your employer to offer support for child care, including on-site child care, referral services, and flexible savings accounts (www.familiesandwork.org).

+ Inform other women about policies that can help with child care costs.

+ Sign up for the National Women's Law Center E-Update newsletter at www.nwlc.org/email, for information about current child care developments and ways to take action.

+ Ask public officials and candidates to support increased investments in child care, and support specific legislation by calling and visiting your representatives and emailing friends and family members about the impending issues.

End the Era of
Latchkey Children

Leslie J. Calman, Senior Vice President, Legal Momentum

In a nation of such prosperity, why are so many of our children being left alone every day? Over 28 million children between the ages of 6 and 17 have either a single parent who works outside the home or two parents who work outside the home. These children need quality care and supervision before and after school, over the summer, and during school breaks.[7] Unfortunately, due to insufficient public funding, over seven million children ages 5 to 14 are left on their own on a regular basis.[8]

All parents want their children to be in a safe environment that teaches and nurtures them. And all children deserve to be cared for by adults who love and understand children and know how to support their development. The unfortunate reality is that too many parents must leave their children alone before and after school so that they can work to put food on the table and a roof over their children's heads. Even for middle-class families, the cost of care can be prohibitive – and quality care is too often unavailable.

The results are not good for children or for communities. The peak hours for children and teens committing crimes and crashing cars, or being victims of crimes and car crashes, are 3 PM to 6 PM on school days. Being unsupervised after school doubles the risk that eighth graders will smoke, drink alcohol, or use drugs.[9] Not surprisingly, polling shows that 87 percent of working mothers say that they're most concerned about their children's safety during the hours after school.[10]

In contrast, quality after-school programs promote interactions between parents and schools, increase student attendance at school, and enable kids to develop skills that are valued in the workplace, such as the abilities to work on diverse teams, to use technology, and to think creatively.[11] What's more, quality programs improve students' academic performance.[12]

Making after-school care available to all of our school-aged children will take a partnership among families, community leaders, employers, and unions. Also, local, state, and national branches of our government will have to reassess the needs of children and treat children's care like the social issue it is, instead of a problem for individual families to struggle with.

This misguided notion – that parents alone should be responsible for providing or arranging for child care – is one of the obstacles to taxpayer support for after-school programs. Complicating the situation further is our culture's negative attitude toward mothers who work outside the home, a judgment that persists even though the vast majority of two-parent families need two incomes to make ends meet. No matter what the arguments against taxpayer-supported after-school programs, though, the fact is that funding these initiatives does more than help children in need – it also saves us all money in the long term.

Many economic-impact studies show that public investment in child care, preschool, and after-school programs yields solid economic returns: to the children who perform better in school, to the millions of families for whom child care is the most costly item in the household budget after rent, to businesses that experience lower absenteeism, and to communities and states that benefit from job creation and from reduced crime.[13]

Safe, quality care will also remove what is perhaps the most significant remaining barrier to women's equality. It will enhance women's ability to advance in their jobs, to contribute to the support of their families, to save toward their futures, to quantitatively contribute to our national economy – and to take exceptional care of their families.

> ⋛ **CALL TO ACTION** ⋜

+ Raise awareness among your friends, family, and coworkers. Get people in your community talking about after-school issues; organize a discussion in your PTA, place of worship, or book club (see Resources).

+ Contact your representatives at local, state, and federal levels. Tell lawmakers that quality after-school care is one of your top priorities — and it should be one of theirs!

- Reach out to local media. Write a letter to the editor, or ask TV and radio stations to air public service announcements about after-school programs.

- Download the Action Kit at Legal Momentum's Family Initiative web-site (www.familyinitiative.org). It's a step-by-step guide that gives you the tools you need to take action now on child care, preschool, and after-school issues. You can also sign up to receive ongoing action alerts.

Guarantee Paid Sick Leave

Rosa L. DeLauro, U.S. Representative

At some point, every working parent has to take time off from work to tend to a sick child, whether because of a cold or a more serious illness. Taking time off is a right that many of us take for granted. But 86 million people in the American workforce do not have that right[14] – a fact many Americans might find shocking. Most of us would agree that being a working parent should not mean having to choose between your job and taking care of your family, but that's what many parents are forced to do each day.

Unlike 139 other nations, the United States does not guarantee paid sick leave to workers – not a single day. The federal Family and Medical Leave Act provides unpaid leave for serious illnesses, but that only covers roughly 60 percent of the workforce. (People who work for businesses with fewer than 50 employees, and most people who work one or more part-time jobs, are not covered by the FMLA.) The result is that working parents, particularly families with incomes under $36,000, have no paid leave of any kind – no paid sick leave, no paid vacation, and no paid personal days.

To correct this injustice, I introduced the Healthy Families Act with Senator Edward Kennedy. Our bill would require employers with 15 or more employees to provide seven days of paid sick leave annually so that the employee can take care of his or her own medical needs or the medical needs of a family member. It would set a baseline for good corporate citizenship.

Working women and their families, in particular, would benefit from paid sick leave. We all know that the brunt of the responsibility to care for children still falls upon women. Half of all working mothers report that they must miss work when a child is sick, and another half of those women do not get paid for the days they miss.[15] Beyond that, nearly a third of all working mothers fear that their colleagues will not be understanding when they miss work and that their job evaluations will suffer as a result of their absence.[16] The legislation we have introduced would bring these working parents something that you simply cannot measure: peace of mind, and the ability to be with their children when those children need a parent most.

The federal government gives its workers 13 paid sick days a year – that's relatively generous compared to the private sector, and it's about the same as many state governments offer their employees. And if those who work for the government are afforded a few days every year to deal with the problems that inevitably come up in daily life, there is no reason in the world that the rest of working Americans shouldn't have this right as well.

It is time our nation recognizes the reality that working parents are the norm in today's society – that employers and employees alike benefit from a workplace that reflects the needs of this sizeable group. Parents should never have to choose between their jobs and their families. Moreover, we know that parents who have not had to make that choice are happier, more productive employees.[17]

The benefits of paid sick leave provided by the Healthy Families Act would give millions of people who are working hard to make ends meet a small modicum of relief when the strain of balancing family and work becomes too much – something that all of us have experienced at one time or another. Helping families achieve that balance is not only a matter of common sense but also one of basic values. And it is time we make it happen.

⋝ CALL TO ACTION ⋜

- ✦ Call or write your representative in Congress and your senators, and ask them to cosponsor the Healthy Families Act.
- ✦ Talk to your family and friends about this much-needed public policy and ask them to do the same.

- ✦ Contact organizations such as the National Partnership of Women & Families (www.nationalpartnership.org), the AFL-CIO (www.aflcio.org), and 9 to 5: National Association of Working Women (www.9to5.org) to volunteer and join the fight to make this legislation a reality.

- ✦ Write your governor and your state representatives to request that they express their support for the Healthy Families Act in writing.

Reform Welfare

Heidi Hartmann, President and Founder, Institute for Women's Policy Research
Cynthia Harrison, IWPR Program Advisory Committee

Too many people, especially politicians, seem to think the U.S. welfare system provides poor women with too much help. In reality, our current welfare system offers only emergency assistance and does so badly. It falls far short of helping poor mothers get back onto their feet. Real welfare reform would attack the root causes of poverty and would create a social safety net that has the potential to enable every American to achieve a decent standard of living and raise a family. The burden of poverty falls most heavily on single mothers with children, who are caught in a system that offers them little and then blames them for not being able to overcome the odds stacked against them.

Despite stereotypes to the contrary, only a small percentage of women enter the welfare rolls as unmarried teenaged mothers.[18] Some women seek help from welfare in order to escape an abusive partner and/or protect their children from an abusive father. Other mothers are disabled or have disabled children. Many mothers work for wages as well, but they cannot make ends meet without additional help.[19]

The women who most often need help are the same ones doing the work our society says we value most – caring for children and helping the elderly. Caregivers who work in the labor market receive the lowest wages among waged workers, and those who attend to their own children's needs are given little economic recognition and no economic security. Most of the jobs poor mothers hold do not entitle them to unemployment insurance, paid sick leave, or paid family leave to care for a new baby. When layoffs, illness, or family needs require that they leave their jobs, most of these women have no personal or job-related safety net.

Until 1996, the federal government ensured poor mothers a small amount of money – the average grant was less than $400 a month – which meant that most recipients still couldn't afford necessities such as a safe place to live. In 1996, only about 4.5 million families (with an average of two children each) were receiving this assistance. Despite welfare's relatively low cost, election-year political conditions in 1996 allowed Congress to enact a much harsher program called Temporary Assistance for Needy Families (TANF).

Rather than seeking to end poverty, TANF focused on cutting welfare rolls, moving welfare recipients into low-wage jobs, and "encouraging" marriage. It permitted states to refuse to assist poor families if they wished, and it limited federal cash assistance to five years regardless of circumstances. Now, although millions of jobs have disappeared, the welfare rolls are still low (only about two million families), meaning that the poorest children and families are not getting the help they need. For example, children in the poorest families, those who earn less than half of what constitutes the official poverty level, are less likely to receive welfare benefits, Food Stamps, or Medicaid now than before welfare reform.[20]

Real welfare reform would seek to end poverty without punitive measures. The limits of the current federal TANF program – and the mandatory work requirements, which are enforced without regard to individual circumstances – should be replaced with a decent level of public support for families in need. As a society, we must provide in-home caregivers with Social Security benefits, and caregivers in the workforce must receive better pay and benefits. Access to education, paid family leave, universal health insurance, federally subsidized child care centers, a guaranteed living wage, and an adequate stock of affordable housing would significantly improve the status of poor women and help them work their way out of the poverty cycle. With the enormous wealth of our country, there's no reason why anyone should be living in poverty.

≥ CALL TO ACTION ≤

+ Contact or meet with your federal and state officials and tell them you want to see TANF modified and genuine welfare measures enacted.

- Write a letter to the editor of local or national newspapers about the need for welfare reform, using the information in this essay and at these websites to inform your letter: www.financeprojectinfo.org/TANF, www.iwpr.org/Poverty/Research_poverty.htm#workwelf, and www.legalmomentum.org/issues/wel/tanf_overview.shtml.

- Go to www.welfarelaw.org/links.html to find a local organization that advocates for poor women in your area and volunteer to help.

Stop Domestic Violence

Lorraine Cole, President and CEO, Black Women's Health Imperative

Every 15 seconds a woman somewhere in this country is punched, slapped, kicked, or otherwise physically abused by a man she knows.[21] By the time you're through reading this essay, more than five women will have encountered a violent attack.

These women are real people, not just statistics. We all know them — they're our beloved family members, friends, and coworkers. All too often, they're ourselves. While our politicians and our media focus on terrorism as the greatest threat to "homeland security," an American woman is most likely to suffer violence at the hands of terrorists she knows — most often male family members or partners.

I've spent many years working to promote the mental and physical health of women. And I've seen firsthand that violence in the home breaks more than bodies — it breaks spirits. Working on an issue that seems so pervasive and widespread can be painful. The sheer magnitude of this epidemic can feel overwhelming. According to the United Nations, one in three women and girls around the world have been physically abused or sexually assaulted.[22] In the United States alone, about 1.5 million women are raped and/or physically assaulted by an intimate partner every year.[23] About half of all American women experience violence perpetrated by men at some point in their lives.[24]

In our culture, domestic and intimate partner violence is a community health crisis that rages among people of all races, religions, and socioeconomic backgrounds. No community is immune, yet each faces unique challenges when confronting this issue. But if we do nothing, statistics show that our silence can be deadly.

Because we lack confidence that our legal system will prosecute or rehabilitate perpetrators of domestic violence, countless women decide not to turn in their abusers. And for too many of us, calling in the authorities puts us in greater danger. Is it any wonder that abused women hesitate to call the police when we consider that more than 17 percent of domestic homicide victims had a protection order against the perpetrator at the time of the killing?[25]

If we do contact authorities, we must cope with very real fears of being attacked further by the court system or the media. Yet the answer to this problem is to improve the legal system, not to circumvent it. When we retaliate with violence, we find ourselves in further peril: many women who are in prison for a violent crime are there for committing retaliatory acts against abusers.[26]

When there is a cultural conspiracy of silence and legal indifference to our plight, it can breed hopelessness. We might blame ourselves and believe that the abuse will stop if we can change our behavior, or we might stay with our abusers out of fear. In order to restore hope and regain our deserved safety, we must take specific actions to slowly change our cultural understanding of abuse, as well as our laws and our attitudes. We can and must put an end to these cycles of violence.

⇒ CALL TO ACTION ⇐

+ Post domestic violence hotline numbers in restrooms, women's publications, bulletin boards, and any other public place where women can see them (see Resources).

+ Learn the signs of domestic abuse so you can provide help to the women in your life (see Resources).

+ Volunteer your time at a local women's shelter. Check "Battered Women Services" in your local Yellow Pages or at www.infousa.com.

+ Donate old cell phones for domestic violence victims to use in emergencies (www.securethecall.org or www.wirelessfoundation.org).

+ Make financial contributions to the National Coalition Against Domestic Violence and the Family Violence Prevention Fund (see Resources).

- Sign up for the online newsletter of Women's Policy, Inc.(www.womens policy.org) or action alerts from the National Women's Law Center (www.nwlc.org).

- Learn about community-based violence prevention and intervention programs at www.pavnet.org.

- Have your book club read and discuss *Black and Blue: A Novel* by Anna Quindlen or *Crows over a Wheatfield* by Paula Sharp. Gather friends and watch the movie *The Burning Bed*. Discuss the real-life implications of these fictional story lines and provide everyone with further resources so they can help families in their lives.

Uphold Peace in Your Community

. . . .

Sarah Harder, President, National Peace Foundation

Since the 9/11 attacks and the U.S. actions in Iraq and Afghanistan, Americans have become particularly conscious of issues of war and peace. This doesn't mean that violence is necessarily more prevalent in the world now than it was in recent history: In the 1990s, 118 wars raged in 80 countries – resulting in the deaths of six million people around the world.[27] But often it is only when the impact of war hits home that we begin to seriously search out peaceful alternatives.

Due to the changing nature of war, which is now fought more often in homes and communities than on battlefields (as evidenced by the Beslan school tragedy in Russia and the genocide in Sudan), women and children make up the majority of war victims and refugees. A recent report by Save the Children, referencing a United Nations study, revealed that in recent conflicts, civilians – the majority of whom are women and children – accounted for as many as 90 percent of all casualties, up from 5 percent at the turn of the last century.[28] This might be one reason why women tend to feel a greater imperative to promote peace. During the chaos of war and displacement, women on the home front must hold families and communities together in order to sustain a measure of stability.

More and more, women all over the world are shedding their roles as victims or spectators, transforming into activists who work locally to prevent conflict, protest war, and rebuild peace. Still, for many of us, the enormous scope and specter of war stand as a daunting barrier to action. We may question whether anything truly effective can be done to promote peace at home, and whether local action can really impact the enormous global changes needed to support postconflict reconstruction and a lasting state of peace.

Yet positive results from local action are possible. When U.S. peace activists gathered one million signatures for the Geneva summit of

Presidents Reagan and Gorbachev, the force of that statement persuaded both Cold War leaders to pursue serious steps toward nuclear disarmament in the 1980s.

Women activists who think globally and act locally favor established strategies that have demonstrated promise for eliminating violence and fostering the practice of peace.

⇒ CALL TO ACTION ⇐

+ Donate your money or time to organizations such as the National Peace Foundation (www.nationalpeace.org) and Women Waging Peace (www.womenwagingpeace.net).

+ Take a stand against violent crimes in your community. Volunteer at your local rape crisis hotline or domestic violence shelter.

+ Call local and national television stations to speak against specific violent images you encounter in the news or regular programming.

+ Participate in or coordinate nonviolent conflict-resolution training in your local schools. For resources, contact the National Peace Foundation: mblakeway@igc.org.

+ Organize conflict-resolution training sessions in your own community, church, or workplace. To learn how, go to the "Workshop on Conflict Resolution" under "Leadership Resources" at the International Federation of University Women's website (www.ifuw.org).

+ Attend or organize community discussions on current conflicts with global implications, such as the Israeli/Palestinian crisis or the Iraq War. You can often find existing discussion groups that are open to the public at local universities, community centers, or religious centers. The National Peace Foundation (www.nationalpeace.org) has further information about how to promote an event in your community.

+ Contact Women in Black (www.womeninblack.net), who have stood publicly and silently for peace since 9/11. Through the group's email alerts, find out what events and activities are happening near you.

3

Grow Your Money, Grow Your Mind

Achieve Higher Levels of Education

Lisa M. Maatz, Director of Public Policy and Government Relations,
American Association of University Women

More women attend college and enter advanced programs of study than ever before. But the statistics detailing women's progress in education don't convey the struggle that many women continue to face in trying to finance and complete their educations. Understanding these challenges is the first step to changing the system and helping women access higher levels of education and achieve financial security and long-term economic independence.

However, in order to obtain this financial security, women must have access to higher education, not just in admissions, but in the financial resources to support them once they enter a program. The economic benefits of higher education are being compromised by the significant debt more and more students accumulate in order to earn their degrees. What's worse, student loan debt disproportionately affects women, who are more likely to borrow than men are and who usually earn less than men, even after college.

Part of the reason women are accumulating increasing debt for their education is that federal loan and grant programs aren't designed to help those who aren't traditional-aged, full-time students. Today, most students at some point will attend school less than half time. This is particularly the case for nontraditional students, who made up 73 percent of college undergraduates during the 1999 to 2000 school year, and who are generally older, financially independent from their parents, and supporting children themselves.[1] Many nontraditional students can only go to school part time while they simultaneously earn a livelihood for themselves and their families. Ironically, despite their hard work, these part-time students don't qualify for stand-alone federal programs and most loan programs. In order to support these nontraditional students, federal student loans should be available to *all* students willing to make a commitment to higher education, even if they have to chip away at that dream one class at a time.

Considerations for determining financial aid must also change. Significant expenses such as child care should be included in the calculations of how much federal financial aid an individual can receive. In addition, policymakers should allow single, financially independent students to keep more of their income when deciding on these students' eligibility for financial aid. Need analyses, which determine aid funding, should reflect the true requirements of these students and their families. We must also support programs that provide guidance, mentoring, and support services for adults reentering college and for other nontraditional students.

Some students do not require a degree or certificate to dramatically increase their earning potential. The Bureau of Labor Statistics has shown that, during the next decade, job seekers will only need a vocational or associate degree in the employment sectors that will grow the fastest. Yet researchers predict that by 2020, 12 million jobs requiring postsecondary training will go unfilled.[2] Many women return to school to refresh their skills or to complete nondegree programs – such as computer science and other high-growth fields – that tend to open doors to better-paying jobs, but they too are faced with economic disadvantages because of the lack of adequate financial support for these kinds of studies. Pell grants and other funding should also be made available to these students.

In order for women to achieve equity both in education and society as a whole, we must make these changes to the financial aid system. Women should not have to sacrifice their education because of policies that limit their opportunities and financial stability.

> **CALL TO ACTION** <

+ Sign up for the AAUW Action Network at www.aauw.org. This email update lets you know when to take action and contact your legislators to support funding for women's education.

- Go to www.aauw.org and order a copy of AAUW's *Women at Work Action Guide*, which offers tools to close the gap between women with resources and those without, to become tech savvy and financially literate, and to fight for better benefits in the classroom and the workplace.

- Fund your college dream. For a comprehensive listing of scholarships specifically for women pursuing undergraduate and graduate degrees, go to www.aauw.org and click on "Fellowships/Grants/Awards." About.com also has a short listing of scholarships just for women (www.collegeapps.about.com/od/women).

Champion Women's Studies

Ellen Boneparth, Director of Policy and Programs,
National Council of Women's Organizations

When, in the 1970s, the pioneer years of women's studies, I coordinated a fledgling women's studies program, I thought of our program as an oasis in the arid sands of the larger university. We provided water, nourishment, rest, and resuscitation for caravans of faculty and students crossing the deserts of patriarchal knowledge. We were doing something new and revolutionary. It took academia a number of years to figure out what it was.

The good news is that today few people still ask the question, "What is women's studies?" Since the founding of the first U.S. women's studies program in 1970 at San Diego State University, the field has mushroomed. Today there are 749 programs in women's studies (sometimes called gender studies) at American universities and colleges. In addition, there are 646 women's centers and women's research centers at U.S. academic institutions.[3] And this does not include the vast number of women's studies programs around the world.

The women's studies field can boast remarkable accomplishments. First, through research, women's studies has established that women are different than men. This may seem obvious, but in academia before the 1970s, it was generally assumed that women were no different than men, and therefore they were not worthy of separate study. We no longer believe that women vote just like men, have identical health problems, or are impacted in the same way by public policy, to name just a few areas in which women's studies research has enlightened us.

Women's studies researchers in every field – especially the social sciences, humanities, arts, and natural sciences – have uncovered extraordinary women whose contributions to civilization were sadly overlooked until recently and who provide inspiring role models for new generations of women and men. Studying the lives of ordinary women is equally important: their struggles to survive and fight oppression make clear that, far from being the weaker sex, women have been the mainstay of the family and a major support for the global economy. We've gained extensive knowledge about women's truths, and there's so much more to uncover.

Women's studies has also raised popular awareness of oppression and difference, not only with regard to gender, but also with regard to race, ethnicity, age, sexual orientation, and religion. Typically, gender discrimination reinforces other forms of discrimination. Using multifaceted analyses has promoted the study of oppressed peoples on all dimensions, not merely gender.

If we've made all of these advancements through women's studies, then what's the bad news? Unfortunately, it's that the need for women's studies is as great as ever. Back in the 1970s, my women's studies colleagues and I believed we would eventually persuade academia to integrate the study of women into all classes on all subjects, thereby eliminating the need for separate study of women's issues and achievements. We expected this because we understood that separate is never equal. Today, with rare exceptions, most courses in traditional disciplines still omit women as topics for study. And because the overwhelming majority of students electing to take women's studies classes are women, the field is unable to fully impact the attitudes and behaviors of male students.

As much of an oasis as women's studies departments have been, it's time for women's studies scholars and students to bring new knowledge into the mainstream curriculum. While this is no easy task, some approaches have proven successful. Courses taught by teams of women and men have resulted in exciting collaborations and the introduction of brand-new materials into general education courses. Seminars and workshops to introduce faculty to women's studies have sometimes ignited in other teachers a desire to learn more and innovate. When this happens, women's studies departments should publicly recognize those departments and faculty who make significant changes, as well as continue to put pressure on those resistant to change.

+ If you teach at any level of education, make sure your courses and those of your colleagues include women's issues and achievements.

+ Students, ask your teachers why women are absent from course syllabi and share your favorite books and articles on women with your teachers.

+ Citizens, ask your elected officials to provide support for the Women's Educational Equity Act (www.ed.gov/pubs/Biennial/125.html).

Demand Pay Equity

Nancy L. Hurlbert, President, Business and Professional Women/USA

Think the wage gap is a thing of the past, or that women earn less solely due to the "choices" they make in selecting a career? Think again. In the last couple of years, numerous wage discrimination lawsuits have been settled in favor of women who haven't received pay equal to that of their male counterparts. Blue-chip companies like Boeing, Morgan Stanley, Coca Cola, and WalMart are just a sample of the businesses being sued for their pervasive pay inequity.

No other single economic factor has a greater impact on the lives of working women than the wage gap. Forty years after Congress passed the Equal Pay Act and Title VII of the Civil Rights Act, women continue to experience wage discrimination. According to figures from the U.S. Census Bureau,[4] women, on average, are paid only 77¢ for every dollar their male counterparts earn. These cents add up to big dollars: for every $10,000 the average man receives, the average woman is paid only $7,600. The wage gap is even worse for minority women; for African American or Latina women, the average compensation is 69¢ and 56¢, respectively, for every dollar of a man's earnings. This gap causes individuals and families to suffer, leaving them with less money to spend on groceries, housing, college funds, child care, and retirement savings.

The first thing that must be done to close the wage gap is ensure that women are well versed in the art of salary negotiation. Women must research the salaries in their fields and ask for fair salaries when they first accept a position. They must also insist that their salary increases are commensurate with cost-of-living increases, increased responsibilities, and high performance.

Business leaders must also recognize that paying women workers unfairly – besides being unethical and immoral – can cost companies much more in the long run. For example, in July 2004, the courts gave preliminary approval to settle a class-action suit against the Boeing company. Approximately 29,000 female employees alleged pay and promotion discrimination, and settling this suit will likely cost Boeing between $40.6 and $72.5 million.

Finally, to achieve pay parity, we as a society must change and enforce laws that mandate equal pay. For example, we must pressure legislators to cosponsor legislation like the Paycheck Fairness Act, which aims to strengthen the Equal Pay Act and closes loopholes that make it easier to pay women unfairly. The proposed law would also make it illegal for employers to fire employees who share their salary data – a crucial provision since women often don't know they are being paid unfairly because they are prohibited from discussing their salaries with coworkers.

The wage gap has only narrowed one half-cent a year over the past 40 years, even though the workforce has been transformed by the influx of women during this same period. At this slow rate of "progress," it will take another 40 years for women to reach wage parity with men. Can we – can America's families – really afford to wait that long?

⊰ CALL TO ACTION ⊱

+ Negotiate for a fair salary. The following websites can help you determine the going rate for your position: www.bls.gov/ncs/ocs/home.htm, www.jobstar.org/tools/salary/sal-surv.cfm, www.workindex.com, and www.wageweb.com.

+ Encourage your company to conduct an internal audit of its pay scales to determine whether or not pay inequities exist. Explain that these audits can be insurance for the future, preventing potential lawsuits and employee dissatisfaction, and suggest that your employer refer to "Ten Steps to an Equal Pay Self-Audit for Employers" (www.bpwusa.org/content/policy/signatureevent/epdaudit.pdf).

+ Inform members of Congress about the great sums of money that are lost in their states and districts every year because women are not paid fairly, and ask them to raise the issue of improving and enforcing pay equity laws.

+ Vote for candidates that actively support pay equity. (Historically, pay equity legislation has been supported only by Democratic members of Congress. Since working women's votes are evenly split between Republicans and Democrats, both parties have an obligation to endorse this legislation and help America's working families.)

Reach Economic Self-Sufficiency

Joan A. Kuriansky, Executive Director, Wider Opportunities for Women

M ore women are working than ever before, including nearly four out of five mothers of school-aged children. Yet too many women are in jobs that do not pay self-sufficiency wages, provide benefits such as health care, or offer job security during economic downturns. Women make up 60 percent of low-wage workers. Because many of these women are single parents who are solely responsible for their families welfare, it is no surprise that nearly one-third of these households live in poverty in the United States. Economic realities for women can change if we, as a country, make a commitment to supporting employer, government, and labor practices that help all workers and their families be financially secure. The first step is to face the facts.

On average, the federal minimum wage covers just 34 percent of a family's basic costs. In many parts of the country, the only way a single mother of three can support her family and achieve basic economic security is to earn an hourly wage of $12 in addition to receiving a whole range of public and work assistance – including subsidized child care, food stamps, housing subsidies, and health coverage for children through Medicaid.[5] The reality is that very few families have access to these benefits, either because they're not eligible for them or because they're not aware of the benefits available.

In order for this situation to change, employers must be required to provide health insurance with minimal copayments, funding for training and education, child care and dependent care benefits, paid family and medical leave, and information about public subsidies that can be added to wages to promote self-sufficiency. Developing top-down policies that advance the economic self-sufficiency of workers is good for employers as well as employees; these measures have been shown to decrease turnover, improve morale, and reduce unplanned and frequent absenteeism.[6]

The government must lead the way in helping to build economic security for low-income people. On a local level, the government can develop criteria to grant or withhold permits, and/or offer tax incentives, to businesses offering self-sufficient wages. Federal, state, and local governments can provide access to affordable education and training opportunities that prepare job seekers for higher-wage jobs. They can also subsidize critical work supports – such as child care subsidies, food stamps, and Medicaid – and change income eligibility requirements in order to reach a greater number of struggling working families.

It's also important for women to take charge of their own economic futures. Female students and workers must invest in themselves by accessing all educational and training opportunities available to them. Unfortunately, many women working at minimum- or low-wage jobs are often working a second or third job just to make ends meet, leaving them with little time and money to pursue career advancement programs offered outside of the workplace. This makes it even more important that young women get sufficient education and training before entering the workforce full time and starting families.

Together we can encourage employers, policymakers, community leaders, and individuals to develop and implement strategies that give women the tools they need to take care of themselves and their families. If we don't make this change, low-income families in our society will be caught in an ongoing cycle of poverty that leads to widespread social problems.

≥ CALL TO ACTION ≤

+ Ask your representatives to support legislation requiring employers to provide health insurance and paid leave and to link their employees to additional support programs and services. Ask them to stand behind laws that provide incentives to employers who offer fair compensation packages to their employees; to support economic development proposals that increase economic and educational opportunities for low-wage workers; and to make public-work supports available and accessible for low-income families.

- Support legislation that increases education and training to prepare women and girls for high-skill, high-wage jobs and that raises the minimum wage to narrow the self-sufficiency gap for low-wage workers.

- Get up-to-date information about how you can support change that will help American families make ends meet at www.SixStrategies.org.

- Volunteer your time at a local women's employment resource center or literacy program.

Consume Wisely

Cathleen Witter, Cochair, Younger Women's Task Force,
National Council of Women's Organizations

Cause marketing. Sounds wonkish, doesn't it? But you've probably encountered this type of marketing more than you think. Ever heard the phrase "shop for the cure"?

Cause marketing occurs when a company gives a portion of its profits to a charitable entity. It's presented as a win-win relationship, because cause marketing not only benefits the charity, but it's also a boon to the company's public image and its sales. Cause marketing tends to be directed toward women, because they're the main consumers of smaller-scale goods such as groceries, cosmetics, and household appliances.

Breast cancer is the poster child of cause marketing. As one of the most common cancers to strike women, breast cancer affects most women's lives in some way.[7] Because of this, many companies market products with the promise to give a portion of the proceeds to help women with breast cancer. Often these products (or their packaging) are pink, a color that has become a recognizable symbol for breast cancer causes. But many advocates are urging women to take a closer look before we "go pink"– it might not be as pretty as we think.

A significant problem with many of these breast cancer marketing campaigns is that corporations are benefiting from them far more than cancer research is. In 2002, Eureka donated $1 to breast cancer research for every WhirlWind LiteSpeed vacuum cleaner it sold. Not only is a dollar less than 1 percent of the cost of a vacuum, but Eureka capped its contribution at $250,000,[8] regardless of how many vacuums the campaign helped to sell. Similarly, since 1997, Yoplait has clamored for consumers to purchase its pink-lidded containers of yogurt and mail the lids back to the company. For each lid received, Yoplait donates 10¢ to the battle against breast cancer.[9] You would have to eat three containers of Yoplait every day during the four-month campaign to raise $36 for the cause. These two corporations are not alone in leading consumers to believe that their purchases are more beneficial to the cause than to the corporation's profit margin.

In addition to being misleading, some breast cancer–focused cause marketing is actually dangerous to women's health. Cosmetic companies have been very public in their desire to sell products for the cause, but they have not been as strident about making their products safe. For example, earlier this year a bill was introduced in the California state legislature (AB 2012) regarding the public's right to know about carcinogenic and reproductive toxins in makeup. The Mary Kay corporation was a vocal opponent of the bill.[10] Many of the very same cosmetics that women purchase "for the cure" contain chemicals that researchers have long suspected of contributing to breast cancer, such as phthalates (thay-lates), chemicals commonly found in nail polish, facial moisturizers, and hand lotions. While phthalates are generally strongly regulated by our government, they are not restricted in beauty products, because cosmetics aren't subject to approval by the U.S. Food and Drug Administration (FDA).[11] Likewise, estrogen-mimicking chemicals known as parabens (pair-a-bens) are the most widely used preservatives in the country, especially behind the cosmetics counter. But studies have confirmed that there is a link between breast tumors and parabens.[12]

Despite these studies, the American Chemical Council (ACC), a group funded by the cosmetics industry, maintains that phthalates and parabens are safe, and opposes efforts to require greater safety testing for consumer products like cosmetics.[13]

Cosmetics companies should stop using these potentially cancer-causing ingredients because safer alternatives are available. In the meantime, we need to stop companies from selling us toxic products under the guise of helping cure cancer. "Pink-washing" a product won't save anyone's life if the contents aren't safe.

+ Read the fine print. If you can't tell where the donation is being directed to, or how much of the proceeds are going to charity, you might want to rethink your purchase.

+ Ask who benefits. Be sure that your pennies are winding up where they can do the most good.

+ Make sure your makeup kit is safe by using the searchable product guide at the Environmental Working Group's online report, *Skin Deep* (www.ewg.org/reports/skindeep/browse_products.php).

+ Go to Breast Cancer Action's website and send an email to cosmetic company executives, asking that they remove harmful chemicals from their products (www.thinkbeforeyoupink.org/Pages/CosmeticEmail. html).

Promote Financial Literacy

Stacey Stewart, President and CEO, Fannie Mae Foundation

"*I'm a teacher's aide. Twenty-nine years old, two kids, no husband. I work hard and put in enough hours so I can pay my rent and make sure my kids are fed and clothed. I earn $20,000 a year, the median income for a woman on her own. According to government figures, that puts me 10 percent above the poverty level.*

"*When I get paid, I go to the check-cashing place, where I spend about $500 a year cashing my checks and sometimes getting payday loans.*

"*When our old TV broke, I stopped at the rent-to-own store just down the street. I ended up paying $800 in rental fees for a TV set I could've bought for 200 bucks cash. But in spite of everything, I pay my bills and manage to put a few dollars away each week. Here's what I'm thinking — maybe when my kids are in high school, maybe then I'll have enough saved to put down on a house. Having a house and building equity, that's what'll get me out of this hole. And with that equity, I'll pay for my kids' college. Then when they start out, they won't have to start out in a hole.*"

This woman is absolutely correct that home ownership has the potential to lift her and her family out of poverty. But unfortunately, even if she continues this way for 10 or 15 more years, scraping and saving and paying her bills on time, it's unlikely she'll ever get a mortgage – all because she's not building any credit history. Our national credit system doesn't capture the financial transactions – paying utility bills, repaying payday lenders, regularly meeting obligations at the rent-to-own store – that could attest to her creditworthiness. She's exiled from the financial mainstream. Lacking a credit history, she lacks the ticket to home ownership.

But this woman, and millions like her, have choices that will better her chance of long-term financial success. She can find a bank that provides free checking. She can learn how to establish – and maintain – a good credit history. She needs just one precious resource: reliable information. She needs an escape from the trap of financial illiteracy.

To avoid financial mistakes – and financial predators – every woman in America needs to be financially literate. This is especially imperative for the 34 million American women who are heads of households. Nowhere is the need for financial literacy greater than among the 11 million single mothers who are raising more than 20 percent of our nation's children. Right now, nearly a third of all women who are heads of households live in poverty.[14]

Financial *literacy* is one of the keys to financial *liberty*. The time has come to put this key in everyone's hand.

≥ CALL TO ACTION ≤

✦ Become financially literate yourself, if you aren't already (see Resources).

✦ Talk to your elected officials about supporting and funding financial literacy training in schools and community centers. Ask them to work toward restructuring our credit system so that it enables more hard-working Americans to earn a credit history.

✦ Demand that financial literacy be a part of our public education curriculum — in every school, available to every student. If local schools are not teaching financial literacy, go to open meetings of the school board and ask if financial literacy can be added to the curriculum. Also ask teachers during parent-teacher conferences. For more information about how to teach financial literacy, go to www.nefe.org and www.fdic.gov.

✦ Talk to your city council and other community organizations about urging mainstream financial institutions to become active in underserved neighborhoods where predatory financial practices thrive. Check-cashing companies make billions of dollars every year performing services that mainstream banks do for free or for a tenth of what these other companies charge.

Advance Women in Business

Hedy M. Ratner, Copresident, Women's Business Development Center

Fairness. When was the last time you heard that term used, especially in the dog-eat-dog, anything-to-make-a-buck world of business? Yet it is simple fairness that will support and accelerate women's business ownership and further strengthen our impact on the economy. Unfortunately, we aren't talking about a remotely fair or equal-opportunity arena, and that is what's holding women back from achieving our full potential.

Still, we've managed to make tremendous progress. In 1973, women owned only 5 percent of our nation's businesses. Today, the ten million women-owned businesses in the United States make up more than half of the businesses in our country. Twenty percent of these businesses are owned by women of color. In total, women-owned businesses generate $2.3 trillion in sales and employ 18.2 million workers.[15]

Despite our successes over the past 30 years, women continue to face blatant discrimination and unwarranted lack of opportunity in the business world. For example, less than 5 percent of all federal government contracts and 3 percent of corporate transactions are awarded to women business owners, and less than 5 percent of all venture capital goes to women-run businesses.[16] And even though we own more than half of our nation's businesses, because of discrimination, our revenues are less than a third of what businesses owned by white men earn.

You might expect that there are laws that support or even mandate access to government contracts for minority- and women-owned businesses – but there are few remaining. In virtually every state, challenges to affirmative action have been waged and won in the courts. Laws that used to force the government to step outside the old boys' network and share the public wealth have been dismantled, and business opportunity programs have been largely eliminated.

The city of Chicago stands as a lonely beacon, continuing to prove that affirmative action does work. This city is one of the few that understands that affirmative action isn't about affording women and people of color unfair advantages, it's about providing them with an equal opportunity. Chicago is successfully monitoring programs through the efforts of a fair-minded mayor (Richard Daley) and a community that has risen to the challenge of fairness and staved off anti-affirmative action litigation. It is the only legally challenged affirmative action program that continues to function.

As if eliminating affirmative action on state and local levels weren't enough, in 2004 the U.S. Small Business Administration (SBA) and Congress eliminated support for virtually all programs that support women- and minority-owned businesses in the United States. What was lost included crucial microlending programs, which provide small loans (under $25,000) to small minority- and women-owned businesses. Across the country, women's-business assistance centers have lost SBA funding, and small-business assistance in economically disadvantaged communities has been cut.

There are plenty of things that can be done to enhance business opportunities for women-owned businesses. Large corporations and government agencies can make concerted efforts toward supplier diversity, allowing more businesses a chance to bid on contracts. Providing greater access to capital for women and minority business owners will also enhance opportunities. Currently, women-owned firms are receiving only 9 percent of investment deals, and only 39 percent of fast-growth women-owned businesses receive commercial bank loans (compared to 52 percent of fast-growth male-owned businesses).[17] These inequities are disturbing, since women-owned business firms are just as financially strong and creditworthy as the average male-owned firm.

Whether you're a business owner yourself, or simply care about equality for women, it's time to take action and join us in the fight for a simple, eight-letter word: fairness.

+ Shop at local women- and minority-owned businesses whenever possible.

+ Follow the news and sign up for action lists that let you know when to speak out about specific legislation. Let your lawmakers know that you support business opportunity programs and that you want your city, state, and national governments to provide equal opportunity to businesses owned by women and people of color.

+ Learn more about how to develop and expand your business with existing resources (www.sba.gov/starting_business/index.html or www.onlinewbc.gov).

Prepare for Retirement

. . . .

Cindy Hounsell, Executive Director, Women's Institute for Secure Retirement

I n the past two decades, our country has experienced a dramatic change in how we're expected to support ourselves during retirement. Increasingly, we are being compelled to bear the risk and responsibility for accumulating the bulk of our retirement income, as company pensions are replaced by savings plans such as 401(k)s. And that's the good news – the bad news is that half of the workforce has no retirement plan at all. As the Social Security system is likely to be reformed to prepare for an aging population, workers are beginning to understand that Social Security benefits were never meant to be the primary source of income but to provide a bare minimum of protection.

These changes in expectation leave many individuals in a precarious position, particularly women living paycheck to paycheck. Women tend to make less money in their lifetimes due to their types of jobs, the lack of pay parity, and the fact that they often must work fewer hours than men in order to spend unpaid time taking care of children and parents. On top of that, women live longer than men, which means that we'll need even more retirement income. The ever-rising costs of medical care, inflation, and the loss of a spouse or partner can also increase a woman's financial burden in later life. The growing incidence of divorce may also have a future financial impact on women, since single women are the most vulnerable to poverty during their retirement years.

Preparing for retirement is the key to economic stability in the later part of your life. Generally, people have no idea how much they'll need to live on when they grow old. The first step is to figure out how much you'll need in your "future paycheck" to pay bills during your postretirement life (which generally lasts 20 to 30 years).

The second step is to figure out where your retirement money will come from. Traditionally, retirement income is a combination of an employer-provided retirement plan (such as a 401[k] or a traditional company pension), Social Security benefits, and your personal savings.

It's never too early (or too late) to take action to improve your financial future. If you can afford to do so, it's important to start saving and investing as early as possible, to take advantage of retirement plans on the job, and to set up and maximize your individual savings plans by contributing to an individual retirement account (IRA). If you are closer to retirement age, you may also benefit from continuing to work as long as possible (currently, Social Security benefits increase by 8 percent for those who delay their retirement past the full retirement age of 66).

President Bush's 2001 Social Security Commission called for a partially privatized individual account system, but critics of privatization are concerned that such a system will lower benefits for women and weaken the long-term financial status of the Social Security system. A main point of disagreement among experts on both sides of the privatization issue is whether there is an immediate crisis and if so how to resolve the crisis. The "no immediate crisis" side of the debate points to the Social Security Trustees' report which shows all benefits can be paid through the year 2042, while the Congressional Budget Office shows 2052 as the projected date.

As an aging society, we must plan for our economic future head-on. It's up to us to speak up about this issue, to our representatives and to the media, before we see a new generation of older women living in poverty.

⇉ CALL TO ACTION ⇇

+ Visit our website (www.wiserwomen.org), a nonprofit resource for financial education and retirement planning information, for help taking the following actions.

+ Review your Social Security statement (sent annually three months before your birthday) and make sure it is correct. Compare it to your W-2 form.

- Consider how changes to Social Security could impact you. Discuss the issue with people you know and call your elected representatives and ask them how they stand on Social Security reform.

- Support care-giving credits for people who take time off work to care for parents and children. These Social Security credits would increase women's retirement income and would benefit up to eight million people. Call your elected representatives and ask for their help. Go to www.iwpr.org for more information.

- Email or call your elected officials to advocate for the renewal of the "saver's tax credit," which provides government-matching funds for low-income workers who contribute to retirement plans at work or to individual retirement accounts that they set up themselves.

- Educate yourself and others about financial planning. When making your retirement plan, try to plan for contingencies such as divorce or the death of a partner, as the majority of women end up single in old age.

4

Lead the Way

Advocate for Women
in the Media

Eleanor Smeal, President, Feminist Majority Foundation

For over 30 years, women have worked to improve our representation in the media. Thanks to decades of feminist activism, we've made tremendous progress. But those advancements are in a backslide that must be stopped.

In the 1970s, the Federal Communications Commission (FCC) had regulations prohibiting sex discrimination and requiring broadcasters to provide programming in the public interest. This included that TV and radio stations had to adhere to equal time provisions, which required broadcasters to show a diversity of views on controversial issues. The regulations, although weak, provided the opportunity for citizens to challenge broadcasting license renewals. Such challenges seldom succeeded, but they could result in delays of license renewals, and the mere threat caused station and network executives to react – and to negotiate. So we feminists challenged away.

Those heady days marked my early work with the National Organization for Women (NOW). In 1971, we challenged the license renewals of the principal TV stations in Pittsburgh, Pennsylvania, on the grounds of sexism. As a result of these challenges, not only in Pittsburgh but also in cities across the nation, NOW activists negotiated agreements with radio and TV stations that led to the hiring of women and minorities, both in front of the cameras and behind the scenes, and that resulted in increased programming for women and minorities. We prevailed through tough negotiations with both television and radio stations.

Meanwhile, women writers "sat in" at national news and women's magazines, demanding and winning more opportunities. At that time, women were often denied bylines and were relegated to the roles of researchers, not writers. Individual feminists sued the wire services, major newspapers, TV networks, and radio and TV stations because of sex discriminatory practices in employment.

The results were slow but stunning. Over time, women working at news magazines won promotions to become reporters, and the careers of major women anchors began. Today, women serve in prominent media roles, as anchors of leading morning TV shows on all the networks and as editors of many national magazines and major newspapers. These success stories, virtually unheard of in the early 1970s, were hard won by dedicated feminists who demanded to see women in positions of authority in the media.

But in the 1980s came the Reagan revolution – and the era of deregulation of the media began with a vengeance. The FCC regulations were gutted. License challenges became more and more difficult and all but disappeared. Finally, the Telecommunications Act of 1996 permitted the wholesale buying of television stations by a few media monopolies and resulted in the creation of six major global media players. Today, two radio conglomerates – Clear Channel and Viacom – control 45 percent of all radio revenues and reach 42 percent of listeners.[1]

Today, we are sorely lacking in strong FCC regulations, competition in media markets is disappearing, and affirmative action requirements for women and minorities in employment no longer exist. The statistics show that the number of women TV correspondents and news directors (positions that are already male dominated by an almost two-to-one margin) is dropping instead of increasing. A 2002 survey of evening news on ABC, CBS, and NBC conducted by Fairness and Accuracy in Reporting showed that the vast majority of U.S. sources interviewed were white, male, and/or Republican (where party affiliation was identifiable). Women make up only one-third of journalists overall, a number little changed since 1982.[2]

In order to reverse the current direction, we must take on the media with public pressure, putting teeth back into the FCC regulations. The public owns the airwaves and must not allow them to be constantly abused with violence, sexism, racism, and homophobia. We must also support feminist media – with so much of the media being taken over by conservative media moguls, we must keep voices of feminism strong on the newsstands, in the classrooms, and in the minds of women and opinion makers. Taking action now will move us toward a media that accurately and positively represents women, minorities, and the issues that impact us most.

≥ CALL TO ACTION ≤

+ Let your senators and representatives know that you oppose legislation that fosters media conglomeration and support regulations that restore the strength of the FCC to counter discrimination and stereotyping.

+ Support feminist publications, such as Ms. magazine, *off our backs*, Women's eNews, *Bitch, Bust, New Moon, FIERCE, Girlfriends, Curve, Hip Mama, Minnesota Women's Press, Lilith*, WINGS (Women's International News Gathering Service), and *Teen Voices* with subscriptions and advertising.

+ Call your radio and television stations to voice your concerns about objectionable programming and advertisements, and to express what you'd like to see. Support feminist columnists and journalists such as Ellen Goodman, Molly Ivins, Barbara Ehrenreich, Katha Pollitt (*The Nation*), Janeane Garofalo (Air America Radio), Terry Gross (*Fresh Air*), and Amy Goodman (*Democracy Now!*).

+ Join the online alert lists of organizations working to reform the media (see Resources) to stay abreast of the latest developments on this issue and learn about the specific actions needed.

Get Every Woman to Vote

....

Kim Gandy, President, National Organization for Women (NOW)

W hen I was in high school, I lost a club election by one vote. Ironically, it was my own: I had gotten the idea that it was prideful
to vote for myself. But as important as an individual vote can be in any
one election, our greatest potential for change lies in combining our votes
into a powerful block that by its sheer numbers can determine the outcome of election after election.

Twenty-two million: that's the number of unmarried women who
didn't vote in the 2000 elections. This is the largest demographic group
in the country that both underregisters and undervotes.[3] Why? Many
mistakenly believe their votes won't matter – but together we have a
tremendous voice, millions strong. Just imagine the difference it would
make if even a fraction of those 22 million women start speaking their
minds by casting their ballots.

On April 25, 2004, more than a million people participated in the
March for Women's Lives in Washington, D.C. A rainbow of faces, every
age and race, from Maine to Nebraska to California, came together for the
biggest demonstration Washington, D.C., has ever seen.[4] Those marchers,
and millions more who were there in spirit, returned home determined
that women's voices would be heard.

After the march, NOW and the NOW Foundation launched voter
education and registration drives, joining scores of nonprofit organizations that together registered and inspired millions to become politically
involved in the 2004 elections. Across the country, volunteers worked
night and day to bring the disaffected, the disenfranchised, and the disil-
lusioned back into full participation in our democracy. We wanted women
to raise their voices by using their votes, and they did. But it can't end with
the last election – there is so much more to do.

So talk to your neighbors, friends, and coworkers! Let them know that
by raising our voices in unison, at the polls, we can begin to make the

changes we want to see in the world. Then none of us will have to wonder what would have happened if we'd only cast our single votes – and none of us should ever hesitate to vote for our own interests. If we don't do it, who will?

⋺ CALL TO ACTION ⋵

+ Go to www.10forchange.org, make sure *you* are registered to vote, and learn how to help others register and get involved.

+ Talk to ten friends, family members, classmates, or coworkers about the importance of their vote in every election and help them get registered.

+ Write a letter to the editor of your local newspaper on the specific importance of an upcoming election or the overall importance of voting.

+ Learn more about the candidates running for office in your area and identify those who support equality and justice.

+ Download fact sheets from www.10forchange.org and ask the candidates about the issues you care about.

+ Volunteer ten hours for voter registration or voter education efforts before each election.

+ Work ten hours on the campaign of a candidate who supports equality and justice for all — or identify a potential candidate who supports your issues (it could be you!) and encourage her or him to run for office.

+ Call all the people you have talked to about issues on the "10 for Change" website to make sure that they vote on Election Day.

+ Help to get out the vote on Election Day. Best of all, volunteer to turn out votes that day for the campaign of a candidate you truly support.

+ Vote!

Nourish Women's Ambitions

Marie Wilson, President and Founder, The White House Project

In 1984, I was working in Iowa as a civic activist and building Drake University's division of women's programming. I was no stranger to leadership. Yet I was surprised when a friend, who was then the only woman serving on the Des Moines City Council, called me with a challenge: "If you don't run for the open seat on the council, I'm going to resign." She was tired of being alone.

I never would have put myself forward if she hadn't picked up the phone, and I went on to win the male-dominated race. In the years since, as I have fought for women's leadership and girls' resiliency, I have thought often of that life-changing call, and how that small act had such a ripple effect through my life and my work.

Many of us need this push to excel, since our society is so ambivalent about our ambition. We are more than 50 percent of the population, yet as of 2004 we comprised only 14 percent of Congress and were only eight of the CEOs at Fortune 500 companies. Today, those in middle management – the majority of future corporate leaders – are about 90 percent male and white. Women have entered the workforce in massive numbers, but most of us remain at the lower rungs of the hierarchy.

Countless published articles have claimed that the primary reason we haven't rocketed to higher ranks is that we just don't want to and that we don't have the same drive men have. That's an oversimplified and sexist explanation. Sure, there are some women who aren't particularly ambitious, but the same thing can be said for some men. The reasons why more women aren't ascending to the highest ranks of corporate and political leadership are complex; they include a heavy dose of good old-fashioned discrimination in the workplace and a second shift where women still shoulder a disproportionate share of work in the home.

Still, we do sometimes hold ourselves back from pursuing our dreams and reaching our full potential. Some of us feel intense guilt for wanting something more than our traditional roles of wife and mother. We're also subjected to a cultural fear that if we focus intensely on our careers, we'll opt not to have families or we'll challenge our traditional roles in them. Because of this fear, society actively tries to limit our choices, refusing to provide child care and new models of corporate success that would allow us to have both a career and a family. Women are still forced to choose between professional success and family life in ways that men are not.

Because of the obstacles in our way, many women need to be entreated to enter public service beyond the home or beyond their current aspirations. I and many of my female colleagues have greatly benefited from getting the right encouragement at the right time. According to research,[5] 37 percent of women who have run for office say they hadn't seriously considered it until someone else brought it up (compared to 18 percent of men who needed prompting). Clearly, our support of each other is powerful.

Let's reach beyond and push the culture to change, one woman at a time. Surely you know someone who should be urged to go back to college, start a business, or run for the school board or Congress or president of the United States. Women are half the population. Let's help run the place, at every level, in every sector. Everyone will be better off.

⋛ CALL TO ACTION ⋚

+ Encourage female friends and family members to stretch themselves and reach their greatest ambitions. Call someone today and offer to support her success by cheering her on, helping out with child care, reading a résumé, or running her campaign.

+ Become a "great mentioner." When you notice someone you think is terrific, tell folks in your circle. Get a buzz going on about her possibilities and drop her name when opportunities arise.

+ Change the country by targeting one woman a month whom you will encourage to run for office. The White House Project (www.thewhite houseproject.org/become_leader/index.html) provides tips and resources. Send her a check as her first contributor, even if it's a small one. It may be the best investment you ever made.

Develop Political Leaders

Karen O'Connor, Women & Politics Institute, American University

In 1999, I attended a two-week intensive leadership program at the Center for American Women in Politics. The program was designed to engage and excite more young women to become involved in politics. As I was standing in a long, slow-moving buffet line, I started talking to the young woman in front of me, a participant in the program, about her reasons for being there.

"So, what about politics interests you the most?" I asked.

"Politics?" she replied. "I hate politics."

Surprised by her response, I asked why she had come to the program, if that was the case. As it turned out, she was there to get the necessary skills to reach her goal of being on the school board to set policy for her kids. She, like so many other young women I've encountered since, say that they're very interested in a range of policies, but at the same time they're dead set against politics. Many young women today fail to see the direct connection between their lives and politics; others simply view politics as too male or too unsavory for them.

The obvious flaw in this stance is that policies are the outcome of a political process. And while many young people have legitimate complaints against the current state of our government and the political process, we must convince them that one of the most effective ways to change the system is from the inside. We must encourage young women to become engaged in politics and to aspire to positions of political leadership. And in their moments of despair about the state of our country and our world, we must remind them that politics is the only way to change the policies that affect them and their communities.

The number of young women currently in political office in our country is far behind the number of young men. In 2004, there were only 2 women members of Congress under age 40, compared to 19 men. In state legislatures, only 12 percent of all state legislators under age 35 were women.[6] And largely because young women don't see themselves represented in our government, only 30.5 percent of women in their first year of college believe that keeping up with politics is essential or very important.[7]

It's no small task to develop and encourage a new generation of female political leaders. Parents, teachers, and larger community and national organizations must all work together to support our girls and young women. For instance, with the help of The White House Project, the Girl Scouts of the U.S.A. have started offering a Ms. President badge to girls to reinforce the importance of political and civic activity, and Mattel has introduced a Madam President Barbie. And a myriad of young women's political leadership training programs are available to help young women build the networks and skills they need to be great political leaders.

We're making headway, but we need to do more outreach to young girls and encourage them to see themselves as future political leaders. This means teaching them about famous American women and their achievements, right alongside discussions of famous men in American history. It involves talking to them about politics and explaining how their involvement can change the world. If little girls stop getting the message that only men can achieve and that politics is a boys club, they'll be much more poised to become the political leaders of tomorrow.

⇉ CALL TO ACTION ⇇

+ Take your children with you when you vote, discuss political events with them, and encourage them to understand and engage with the political process.

+ Encourage your daughters, young coworkers, or other women to get involved in politics.

+ Join organizations such as the Women Under Forty Public Action Committee (WUF PAC; www.wufpac.org), designed to elect more young women to office.

+ Participate in one of the many young women's leadership training programs offered nationwide (www.american.edu/wandp).

- Sign up for one of the women's leadership training programs hosted by women's groups including the YWCA (www.ywca.org), EMILY's List (www.emilyslist.org), and the National Federation of Republican Women (www.nfrw.org).

- Provide leadership opportunities for young women within your own organizations.

Run for Office

Dianne Feinstein, U.S. Senator

W hen I first ran for the Senate in 1992, there were only two women in the Senate. At the time I said, "Two percent may be good enough for the fat content in milk, but it's not enough for the representation of women in the United States Senate."

Today, there are 14 women senators, which is quite an improvement, but it's still not enough. Worldwide, the United States ranks 58th when it comes to the representation of women in the lower or single parliamentary house. We need to encourage more intelligent and honorable women to run for public office, and then we need to help them win.

Too often women ask: Why should I run for office? Why should I try to make a difference? The answer is: if you are committed to serving the public, you can make a difference and better your and your children's lives, as well as the lives of those in the community for whom you are working.

Women bring a fresh perspective to many issues. Perhaps this is because we have a different set of experiences, or perhaps it is because we simply don't feel bogged down by doing things the way they've always been done.

In my time as a senator, we've made remarkable progress in the political arena. Many issues that were left on the back burner by men have been brought to the forefront by women. Since 1992, we have dramatically increased funding for breast cancer research and domestic abuse shelters, passed the Family and Medical Leave Act and the Violence Against Women Act, and required health insurance companies to cover more health costs that specifically affect women.

Though a career in politics is by no means easy, it can be very rewarding when you know you are doing your best to represent the interests of the people who elected you. If you are interested in working in politics, go for it – be informed, get involved, and stand up for what you believe in.

Many of us choose a career for the wrong reasons – because someone else wants us to, because we want to make the most money possible, or because of societal pressures to do what we think is expected of us. Instead, we each need to turn inward for answers, determine our strengths, gain the necessary education, and steadily work toward our goals. Doing what we do best will enable us to enjoy our work and cast aside disappointment or ignore slights and move on.

In politics, as in any endeavor, it is important to develop strong determination. Hopefully, you will encounter many successes, but you can also expect to encounter setbacks along the way. Staying positive and continuing to move forward will help to sustain any successful career.

I believe that anyone who runs for office should develop an area of expertise that interests her or him. A study of the postconviction phase of the criminal justice system led to my first appointment to the California parole board by governor Pat Brown in 1960, and a lifelong interest in the criminal justice system took root. That interest led me to be the first woman to serve on the Senate Judiciary Committee, and I am now the ranking member of the Terrorism, Technology, and Homeland Security Subcommittee.

There are many reasons to run for office – civic duty, a personal call to service, fame, influence. Think hard about what you hope to accomplish and do what is best for you. Do it for your country. Do it for the people you will represent. Do it for yourself.

⋝ CALL TO ACTION ⋜

+ Stay informed. Read newspapers and other news sources. Follow current events and share information with others.

+ Learn about the issues that impact your community. Know who your public officials are and what offices they hold.

+ Get involved. Go to public meetings of your local government. Join a civic or advocacy group that works on issues important to you.

+ Learn the ropes by volunteering for the campaign of a candidate or cause you believe in.

+ Just do it. Run for office in your local community, city, state, and beyond.

Recognize Women in the Military

Captain Lory Manning, USN (ret.),
Women's Research and Education Institute

There they are – on your TV screen, on the front page of your morning paper, on the cover of national magazines. Sometimes you have to look closely to see that the soldier you're looking at is a woman – sometimes you might feel startled, even shocked, at what she is doing.

In an unofficial capacity, women have served in the U.S. military since the American Revolution. Our official military role began in 1901 with the establishment of the Army Nurse Corps. And by 2003, women made up 15 percent of the active duty force serving in the four Department of Defense services. We also made up 10.7 percent of those serving in the active Coast Guard and 17.2 percent of the force serving in the National Guard and reserves.[8]

Over the last 20 years in particular, military women have made tremendous progress toward equality with military men. Today, women serve in all military units and occupations (including commanding officer) aboard Navy and Coast Guard ships. Women fly, crew, and maintain every variety of military aircraft, in addition to deploying with Army and Marine Corps units around the world.

But despite all the places you can find women in the military, sexism continues to keep women from serving in submarines and ground combat units – no matter how qualified and competent they are, nor how willing to put their lives on the line for our country. This ban continues to be enforced by military policy and the presumed support of these policies by Congress. Additionally, gay men and lesbian women cannot serve openly in the military. The "Don't Ask, Don't Tell" rules place a difficult burden on them, their partners and family.

It's not just individual women's careers that would benefit from female participation in the full range of military service. Women's presence in military operations worldwide enables us to approach problems in uniquely effective ways. For instance, according to press reports, women service members sometimes accompanied special forces on missions in Afghanistan to gather intelligence from the local population; this would be a logical tactical decision, since most rural Afghani women won't speak with men to whom they are not related.[9] Also, according to Dr. Gerard DeGroot of the University of St. Andrews in Scotland, women in peace-keeping forces are "not only better able to control violent tendencies, but are also perceived as less of a threat by the local population and therefore less likely to provoke violence."

Despite their usefulness and dedication, women in the military can face sexual assault and sexual harrassment. It is especially important for civilian women, who confront so many of the same issues, to support their female service members.

⋛ CALL TO ACTION ⋜

Contact your representatives and write letters to the editor in support of these changes:

+ Stop sexual assault of military women by their fellow soldiers and thoroughly investigate and preserve evidence where sexual assault does occur. Demand that the military develop an official support system for survivors of assault and abuse.

+ Revoke policies that discriminate against women (such as the ground-combat and submarine-service bans) and against men (such as the males-only draft registration requirement).

+ Repeal the "Don't Ask, Don't Tell" law so that lesbian and gay service members — who are currently serving by the thousands — can serve openly.

+ Ensure that women veterans, especially those who have served in

---

combat zones, have access to veterans' medical, rehabilitative, and vocational services of the same caliber and geographic proximity as their male peers.

+ Learn more about the issues facing women in the military (see Resources).

Equalize Constitutional Rights

Carolyn B. Maloney, U.S. Representative

The Equal Rights Amendment: Did it ever pass? Is it part of our Constitution? Most Americans aren't sure where our country stands on this important civil rights issue. Seven out of ten Americans surveyed think that the Constitution makes it clear that men and women are entitled to equal rights.[10] Unfortunately, 70 percent of Americans are wrong. The ERA has not yet become law.

If you aren't sure what exactly the ERA will do, read the following, which is the complete text of the proposed amendment:

Section 1. Equality of rights under the law shall not be denied or abridged by the United States or by any state on account of sex.

Section 2. The Congress shall have the power to enforce, by appropriate legislation, the provisions of this article.

Section 3. The amendment shall take effect two years after the date of ratification.

In 1982, when the ten-year ratification period expired, the ERA was three states short of passing. Fortunately for the nine out of ten Americans who believe that the Constitution should state that men and women are entitled to equal rights,[11] the effort to gain constitutional equality is still going on. I coordinate a weekly conference call with experts in a number of different fields to work toward ratification in the 15 states that have yet to ratify the ERA. The ERA has been reintroduced into nearly every session of Congress since 1982, and I am proud to have introduced it since 1997.

Women have advanced a great deal since the ERA was first introduced into Congress in 1923. However, the obstacles to full equality are still substantial and serious. Women continue to earn less than men, earning 77¢ for every dollar that men earned in 2002, according to U.S. Census data. We continue to be underrepresented in many powerful and high-paying fields; while we constitute 47 percent of the labor force in the United States, only eight women head a Fortune 500 company.[12] The United States ranks 60th in the world in terms of female political representation, with women making up only 14 percent of the legislators in the House of Representatives and Senate.[13]

Many critics suggest that there is no longer a need to amend the Constitution to protect women's rights. They argue that the 14th Amendment protects women's rights, even though the 14th Amendment has not always been interpreted to apply to women and has in fact only been applied to sex discrimination since 1971. In our Constitution, the terms "citizens" and "persons" did not, and were not meant to, include women. Based on the courts' interpretations of women's role in society, women were denied the right to vote until passage of the 19th Amendment in 1920.

Equal rights for women were not then, and are not now, protected by the Constitution. Amending the Constitution to clearly define equality between men and women would protect against the possibility of a future Congress or future courts reversing advances in women's rights. Judges and elected officials come and go, but the Constitution remains. We cannot continue to rely on a patchwork of legislation to protect and defend our rights. With the ERA in the Constitution, it would be clear that our society, for all time, rejects acts of gender discrimination and supports equality of rights for men and women.

Alice Paul, suffragist and the author of the Equal Rights Amendment, said in 1923: "We shall not be safe until the principle of equal rights is written into the framework of our government." When I look at my two daughters and think of the future, I know we can't wait any longer. More than 80 years after the ERA was first introduced in Congress, it is time for women to have an equal place in the Constitution.

+ Contact your senators and representatives to encourage them to cosponsor the Equal Rights Amendment (http://clerk.house.gov/members/index.html).

+ Visit www.house.gov/maloney for more information on the ERA.

+ Watch *Iron-Jawed Angels*, the HBO-produced film about women's history and the right to vote.

+ Talk to your friends about the importance of passing the ERA. Send an email to people you know asking them to support the amendment.

Reassess National Priorities

Susan Shaer, Executive Director,
Women's Action for New Directions (WAND)

When it comes to the federal budget, Gloria Steinem said it all: "The federal budget is a statement of our nation's moral character."

On a personal level, your checkbook says a lot about who you are. People spend money on the things they care about. The same is true for countries. The federal budget, our national checkbook, reflects the needs and values of our nation and speaks volumes about the kind of people we are.

In your personal budget, you likely have money set aside for mandatory expenses, such as housing and food and utilities. If you have money left over from your mandatory expenses, what is left are your discretionary funds: money to go to the movies, to pay for cable TV, or to take a nice vacation.

In a similar fashion, the federal budget includes both discretionary and mandatory spending. Discretionary spending, about one-third of the total budget, is determined each and every year through 13 separate appropriations bills. Mandatory spending happens automatically and includes entitlements such as Social Security, Medicare, food stamps, federal pensions, interest payments on the national debt, etc. Mechanisms exist for adjusting mandatory spending, but they are rarely exercised, as these programs are not required to be adjusted every year.

This leaves services and issues such as the military, homeland security, education, job training, environment, health care, housing, international aid, and energy to vie for their piece of the discretionary budget. For example, when military spending grows, it is often at the expense of other slices of the pie that also rely on federal money. The fiscal year 2005 budget proposal ended or cut back 128 programs, including child care, housing assistance, school counselors, employment services, clean air and water, and health care.

It's our money and our services. We should passionately and vociferously care, making our voices heard, so that the budget reflects the collective priorities of all citizens in the country – and ensures that we are spending money on the issues and services that matter most to all of us.

For example, the Pentagon budget for fiscal year 2005 is about $450 billion. Every citizen should know a few facts about that mind-boggling number:

+ $450 billion is over half of the entire discretionary budget.
+ $450 billion is roughly equal to the combined military spending of every other nation in the world. The second-biggest spender is China, at $51 billion. Iran spends $5.1 billion.[14]
+ The $450 billion Pentagon budget contains very little money for homeland security. Homeland security is primarily a function of state and local governments and of federal agencies outside the Department of Defense.
+ The current $450 billion Pentagon budget includes $25 billion for military operations in Iraq and Afghanistan, but most war costs in the year 2005 and beyond – as much as $75 billion – will come from additional "supplemental" requests the president makes to Congress, above and beyond the $450 billion. That money will be added to the deficit, requiring higher interest payments on the national debt. In turn, that means less money to spend on other critical federal priorities.

We're a great nation, but we can always do better. We can meet the security challenges of the 21st century while at the same time ensuring that the basic needs of our citizens, such as food and health care, are met. Elected officials consistently tell us that they need to hear more from constituents about the issues they care about most. They say there is little political pressure on them to put federal dollars toward unmet human and environmental security needs, while they're under immense pressure to increase Pentagon spending and cut taxes. It's crucial that you let members of Congress know what you value. Open the national checkbook. See what's there. Join us in working for change.

+ Elect women to public office. Women generally vote more progressively than men.

+ Contact your elected representatives. Tell them about specific needs in your community. Question rising Pentagon spending.

+ Organize a letter-writing group to write letters to the editor and elected officials.

+ Support WAND (www.wand.org) and other nonprofit organizations working for change (see Resources).

+ Leaflet in front of public buildings.

+ Spend at least some time each week learning more about the issues. Read the news, attend lectures and community forums, and sign up for WAND's email news bulletin at www.wand.org.

5

Forge a Path for the Next Generation

Mentor Women and Girls

Alison Stein, Founder, Younger Women's Task Force

When I graduated from the University of Pennsylvania in 2003, I was confronted with one of the bleakest job markets in recent years. And yet my male friends were getting jobs and my female friends were not. I felt discouraged and hopeless, but I also felt enraged. What was going on? Have we not freed ourselves from the old boys' club that plagued our mothers and grandmothers?

At the University of Pennsylvania, like many major colleges and universities, almost twice as many men as women play an organized sport or are a part of the Greek fraternity system. These informal social networks serve as the ticket for many men to gain entrance into prestigious law firms, financial firms, and consulting firms. My closest male friend, a member of Penn's largest fraternity, received a much sought-after investment banking job from an older fraternity brother without even interviewing with the firm.

"Networking was one of the strongest reasons why I joined my fraternity," he recently explained to me. "I used my fraternity to help me get a job. And I gave back. Every year I have worked at my bank, I have gotten at least one fraternity brother a job."

These informal networks are not as established for women. I interviewed dozens of women who work in finance, consulting, law, and the nonprofit sector. Not one woman could name someone who helped her get her job. But what is even more alarming is that not one of those women has gone on to help another woman get a job even after they secured employment themselves.

"Every woman who achieves any position in an organization where she can mentor a younger woman and bring more women on board has a responsibility to do so," said Martha Burk, a leader in the feminist movement. "This is what men have been doing forever and that is why they remain in control."

In addition to aiding with career development, mentors can provide a model for the diversity and balance required in women's lives. Many young women learn just as much or more from their female mentor's lifestyle and life choices as they do from their professional experiences.

"Mentoring as many young women as possible is what we can do to make sure young women realize they have choices and have all the opportunities that men do," said Ellen Boneparth, a former women's studies professor. "For example, if our goal is to get equal numbers of women in politics, I have to mentor young women and convince them that if they want to, they can run for political office."

An older woman can also benefit from a relationship with a younger woman. Besides a fresh outlook, younger women often bring technological skills, significant educational experience, and an understanding of popular culture and current trends to the relationship. In fact, many psychologists prefer to use the word "co-mentoring," which implies a collegial relationship between mentor and mentee.

"As a professional women, mentoring is probably the single most important thing I do," said a woman who directs an organization. "You have such long-term impact, but you also learn a tremendous amount with each mentoring experience."

Once I actively sought out and built a relationship with the woman who is now my mentor, I was finally able to find a job. By teaching me how to merge the personal and professional parts of my life, she has become my model of balance and my own daily reminder of both the challenges and the possibilities that lie ahead.

≥ CALL TO ACTION ≤

+ If you are a woman who has established herself in her profession, ask yourself at the end of every week what you have done to bring another young woman on board. If you can't hire another woman, mentor younger women in your organization.

+ If you are a younger woman launching your career, join an intergenerational organization that provides you with community and networking opportunities (www.mentors.ca/mentorlinks.html). Actively seek out a mentor in your field whom you respect and admire.

+ Participate in a summer internship or a fellowship program that provides young women with leadership training and skill building (see Resources).

Teach Honest Sex Education

Martha E. Kempner, Director of Public Information,
Sexuality Information and Education Council of the United States

Since 1996, the federal government has sunk over $900 million into programs that tell young people that sexual relationships outside of marriage are *likely* to have harmful physical and psychological consequences. Although referred to as "abstinence-until-marriage programs," they teach a lot more than "just say no"– especially on the topic of gender.

You might be surprised at the extent to which the curricula for these programs refer to outdated social norms and reinforce sexist stereotypes. The student workbook *Sex Respect*, for example, suggests that young people ask for their parents' opinions on whether it is appropriate for girls to ask guys out.[1] *Reasonable Reasons to Wait* asks young people to consider this question: "Will the wife work after marriage or will the husband be the sole breadwinner?"[2] And *Art of Loving Well* asks them to "think of the enormous wisdom contained in the fact that in a wedding ceremony the father 'gives away' his daughter."[3]

Sex Respect anticipates that students will ask the bizarre question: "Are boys who abstain really considered 'virgins'?" The answer the book provides: "Although the term more commonly is used in reference to girls, it applies to boys too."[4] While at some distant point in our cultural history, the word "virgin" might have only referred to women, this is no longer the case. By including this as a likely question, the curriculum is subtly reinforcing a model of gender inequality that requires chastity and purity in women but not men.

Gender inequality is further reinforced in discussions of sexual relationships, in which the curricula promote the age-old stereotype that men use love to get sex and women only have sex to feel loved. *Sex Respect* explains that "a young man's natural desire for sex is already strong due to testosterone, the powerful male growth hormone. Females are becoming culturally conditioned to fantasize about sex as well."[5]

By promoting such ideas, these curricula ultimately put the responsibility for controlling sexual behavior on young women. *Reasonable Reasons to Wait* explains, "Girls need to be aware they may be able to tell when a kiss is leading to something else. The girl may need to put the brakes on first to help the boy."[6] Presenting these stereotypes and myths as universal truths can limit the options of young women, influence their behavior, and color the expectations of both girls and boys for future relationships.

Perhaps even more alarming, however, is that these programs present equally biased information about pregnancy- and disease-prevention methods. Young people are told that condoms break, tear, and have large holes; that birth control is difficult to use; and that sexually transmitted diseases (STDs) are simply the inevitable consequence of premarital sexual activity.

It is important for us to remember that by their senior year, 62 percent of high school students in the United States have had sexual intercourse.[7] Telling these students that condoms and contraception do not work will not prevent them from engaging in sexual behavior. It may, however, prevent them from protecting themselves when they do.

Abstinence-until-marriage programs are not new; in fact, they have been around for over two decades. Still, there are no studies in professional, peer-reviewed literature that prove these programs help young people avoid unintended pregnancy and STDs. In contrast, numerous studies have shown that comprehensive education about sexuality – which includes teaching about both abstinence and disease prevention – can help young people delay sexual intercourse, reduce the frequency of intercourse, reduce the number of sexual partners they have, and increase condom and contraceptive use.[8]

We can and must provide our young women with something better than stereotypes, myths, and misinformation.

+ Protest funding for unproven and potentially harmful abstinence-until-marriage programs. Write letters to the editor and call your representatives in opposition to these programs. Ask friends and family members to do the same. See www.nonewmoney.org for more information and advice on advocacy efforts.

+ Ask your elected officials to fund and promote comprehensive sexuality education.

+ Help young people develop the critical thinking skills they need to question the nature, validity, and origin of gender myths, stereotypes, and biases. See www.familiesaretalking.org for information and advice on talking to children about sexuality-related issues.

Liberate Girls from Abuse

Jill J. Morris, Public Policy Director,
National Coalition Against Domestic Violence

Our society supports a myth that domestic violence doesn't affect the children as much as it does the parents. However, studies show that between 40 and 60 percent of men who abuse their partners also abuse children.[9] Despite this statistic, family court judges frequently award fathers sole or joint custody in custody disputes where there is a finding of abuse.[10] While the rationale for these decisions is often that children are better off having a relationship with both parents, there is strong evidence to suggest that allowing an abusive parent visitation or custody rights simply permits the cycle of abuse to continue. One study found that, during visitation, 5 percent of abusive fathers threaten to kill their children's mother, 34 percent threaten to kidnap the children, and 25 percent threaten to hurt the children.[11]

Growing up in an abusive family, and in a society that tries to ignore this abuse, continues to impact children as they grow into young adults. An alarming number of teens are beginning to experience violence in their own relationships. Twenty-six percent of high school girls have been the victim of physical abuse, sexual abuse, or date rape at the hands of their partners.[12] In particular, pregnant adolescents face a greater risk of violence at the hands of their partners than adult pregnant women do.[13]

Many young women think that dating violence is a normal part of growing up or that the violence is just their partner's way of expressing love. It's difficult enough for these girls to get support for physical and sexual violence, let alone have their verbal and psychological abuse taken seriously. However, many victims report that name-calling and verbal attacks affected them as severely as physical abuse.

Young women suffering from violence at home or in their relationships use the same methods of concealing their abuse. They do so because they fear further violence and shame, or they worry that no one will believe them. Abused young women often think that they deserve what is happening to them or that it is a "normal" part of relationships. They also fear the potential loss of family or the breakup of their relationship. This makes it all the more important that parents and others in the lives of young women take note of warning signs and help educate girls on how to avoid or escape abusive situations. If we don't, these young women often give up hope, and many run the risks of running away from home or hurting themselves.

In addition to liberating our girls, we must also help our boys to be caring partners. Today, abusive boys are often excused for their behavior. Many of these boys were themselves victims of or witnesses to domestic violence. These young men need services and programs to help them learn nonviolent skills and to seek counseling for their own victimization.

Breaking the cycle of violence at an early age enables the prevention of future violence. As individuals and as a society, we must do everything possible to protect women and their children from abuse. If we don't, the cycle will never end.

⋝ CALL TO ACTION ⋜

+ Discuss violence and healthy relationships with your children and teens, as well as friends and neighbors. Encourage them to speak up if they think or know that someone is experiencing violence or abuse (see Resources).

+ Get involved with local education and prevention programs. Volunteer with a program to speak at local schools. Insist that schools discuss violence and healthy relationships in their curricula.

+ Support organizations that encourage men to work in ending violence against women (www.menstoppingviolence.org).

+ Do not be afraid to call local hotlines or the police if you suspect someone is a victim or perpetrator of violence.

+ Write letters to local legislators and to Congress appealing for increased funding for violence prevention and education programs and services.

+ Work with local policy groups to ensure that your state domestic violence laws include stalking and dating violence in their statutes.

+ Go to www.ncadv.org for more information on domestic violence programs, services, and public policy.

Support Girls and Women in Sports

Donna A. Lopiano, Chief Executive Officer, Women's Sports Foundation

In 1972, Title IX, a federal law mandating equal opportunity for women in sports, was adopted by Congress. Since that time, the American public's support of girls' sports participation has grown dramatically. Today, among the Americans who know about the law, an estimated 70 percent support Title IX.[14] And as we look toward building a new women's movement, 41 percent of women consider increasing the number of girls who participate in organized sports a top priority.[15]

This widespread support for equal treatment of males and females in sports is directly related to the increased understanding that sports and physical activity are not just about fun and games. According to research, regular participation in physical activity during childhood and adolescence promotes the development of positive body image, confidence, and self-esteem. Girls who participate in sports and physical activity are more likely to graduate from high school, matriculate in college, and experience greater career success. And the health benefits are numerous; participation in sports and other physical activities can help reduce a girl's health risk for obesity, diabetes, heart disease, osteoporosis, breast cancer, depression, unintended teen pregnancy, anxiety and lack of self-esteem, among others.[16]

Participation in sports and regular physical activity have the power to turn around some dire health and wellness statistics for the girls and women in our society. Right now, one in six girls are obese or overweight,[17] four in ten girls get pregnant by the age of 20,[18] and one in three adolescent girls experience depression,[19] anxiety, or eating disorders.[20] One in three girls in high school currently smoke;[21] not coincidentally, lung cancer is the leading cause of cancer deaths among women.[22] And girls aged 4 to 19 have significantly higher "bad" cholesterol levels than boys;

notably, heart disease is the leading cause of death among American women.[23]

In addition to their health benefits, sports also contribute to women's career success. Eighty percent of women who have been identified as key leaders in Fortune 500 companies participated in sports during their childhood and described themselves as one-time "tomboys."[24] More than four out of five executive businesswomen (82 percent) played sports growing up – and the vast majority say that what they learned on the playing field about discipline, leadership, and how to have a competitive edge has contributed to their success in business.[25]

But despite these obvious benefits and widespread public support, we're not succeeding in getting enough girls to participate in sports. Girls don't just need encouragement; they need opportunity. High school boys receive 40 percent more chances to play varsity sports than girls, with similar statistics found on the college level.[26] Our schools and colleges are not complying with Title IX; many contend that they do not have the financial resources to do so. Federal enforcement of the law has been almost nonexistent.

The first thing we need to do is introduce girls to sports at a young age (studies show that if a girl does not participate in sports by the time she is 10 years old, there is only a 10 percent chance she will participate when she reaches age 25).[27] And then we need to continue to support girls throughout their adolescence; by the age of 16, only one in seven girls attend physical education class daily, and a startling 15 to 30 percent report that they engage in no regular physical activity at all.[28] As parents, educators, and community members, we must act to improve these numbers. The health and success of tomorrow's women depend on it.

≥ CALL TO ACTION ≤

+ Pledge to help one girl get active over the coming year. Learn how to inspire and motivate sedentary girls at GoGoGirl (www.gogogirl.com).

+ Make a difference for girls in your community by finding out whether

---

your school or college athletic program is complying with Title IX. Go to Geena Davis's website (www.GeenaTakesAim.com) for information about actions you can take.

+ Take young girls to women's sports events so they can discover strong and healthy role models.

+ Contribute to a girl-serving organization to make sure that under-served girls and girls from economically disadvantaged households have a chance to play.

+ Be physically active yourself so that you're a role model for the girls in your family; it's important for girls to see women moving and enjoying physical activity.

Celebrate Women's Achievements

Molly Murphy MacGregor, President and Cofounder,
National Women's History Project

In 1980, less than 3 percent of the content of teacher training textbooks had information related to women. More than 20 years later, in 2002,[29] a study of teacher training textbooks demonstrated that the content *about* women in teacher training textbooks still remained the same – at less than 3 percent. Clearly, our teachers and children aren't learning about women's extraordinary contributions to our society, our culture, and our history.

Certainly, progress in raising the visibility around women's successes has been made. The celebration of National Women's History Month each March has helped lend some color to the previously invisible ink in which women's history has been written. But the effort to gain full acknowledgment for our achievements needs to be ongoing. We need to continue to challenge entrenched stereotypes that define women as passive nonparticipants in the major ideas and decisions that shape culture and history. These assumptions, often unconscious, are held by men and women alike. Studying family, community, state, national, or world history from the perspective of women's achievements presents a more accurate picture of women's tenacity, strength, and talent.

As the cofounder and president of the National Women's History Project (NWHP), I have worked with thousands of school districts and women's organizations throughout the country. In 1999, I was appointed by the White House to the Women's Progress Commission, a congressional commission authorized to study women's historic sites in the United States. Our findings were distressful. Women's landmarks and women's historic sites are disappearing at an alarming rate, and restoring them is an expensive endeavor. Women's historic achievements are often undervalued, or not recognized at all, and preservation of our valuable history is all too often not a priority in our society.

We must all become involved in saving our history – for ourselves, and for our children. We need to bestow on the children of the United States the knowledge of our complex and rich history. They need to know the problems that Americans have faced, solved, and ignored, as well as the stories of everyone who helped create the rich, diverse culture of this country. They also need to understand the essential role women have played in history. Not teaching children about the courage, determination, strength, and intelligence of our nation's women leaves students – male and female – with the impression that women have not been active participants in our nation's history.

Learning women's individual stories provides a much larger perspective on our nation's history and offers women and girls greater confidence and a sense of infinite possibility. Teaching these stories to new generations has the power to challenge sexist and racist stereotypes and to prompt our children to value equality. Our children's sense of possibility can only grow with the inspiration that comes from knowing our history.

≥ CALL TO ACTION ≤

+ Write to your state board of education and encourage its members to require curriculum that covers women's contributions to history, literature and the arts, and math and science. Visit NWHP's website (www.nwhp.org) and go to the "Learning Place" for sample letters and curriculum ideas.

+ Encourage your local school district to celebrate March as National Women's History Month, and offer to help organize speakers or assemblies that teach kids about women's achievements. NWHP's Women's History Month page offers tips on how to organize such events.

+ Make sure your children's schoolwork equally emphasizes women's contributions to each subject. Provide overworked teachers with resources to help them supplement curriculum.

- Encourage your city council to develop historic sites that celebrate women.

- Visit historic sites dedicated to women. Find out more information from National Collaborative for Women's Historic Sites (http://ncwhs.oah.org).

- Create a book group dedicated to reading biographies about women and their amazing accomplishments — these books make great reads and are sure to inspire you and your friends.

- Visit www.nwhp.org for information and resources about women's historic accomplishments and for strategies on how to spread the word.

- Don't give up. It took 72 years for women in the United States to win the right to vote, but those activists did eventually create tremendous social change.

Gain Daily Access to Science and Technology

Shireen Mitchell, Executive Officer, Digital Sisters

W hen the first computer was built, it was as big as a warehouse room and was worked on mainly by women "computers," whom we know today as "programmers." Six of the nine programmers were women, who were considered to be the best people for the job because of their patience, accuracy, and critical thinking.[30] Today, however, many assume that women and girls aren't good at or interested in science and technology. As technology has become a male-dominated big business, profits have been prioritized over accuracy, and the unique skills women bring to the table have increasingly been undervalued.

Prior to the fourth grade, girls are as interested in technology as boys, studies have shown. After that, girls find themselves discouraged by the adults in their lives and constantly challenged by the boys in their class, which tends to turn them away from pursuing the subjects of science, math, and technology.[31] Adolescent boys are more actively encouraged by teachers, parents, and manufacturers to engage with technology; they're more often asked by teachers to assist in technology-related projects or to help others in the classroom, and they're often allowed to monopolize family computers in the home. Adolescent girls are intensely pressured to be "cute" instead of "smart," which directly conflicts with our cultural preconceptions that tech geeks and scientists are awkward or stuffy.

With this unappealing model, and a dearth of female role models in the field, teen girls often fail to even consider technology as a career option. The majority of teen girls opt out of classes in science and technology when allowed to do so. By neglecting to explore these subjects in high school, many young women find it difficult, if not impossible, to apply for certain degrees or jobs. Already, lack of technological skills is one reason why women involved in Welfare to Work programs aren't able to find jobs paying more than entry-level salaries. If not addressed, the lack of technological training will lead to an even greater lack of job opportunities for women over time.

Without better technological training and awareness, women will also be susceptible to the increasing dangers of technological illiteracy. We'll be unprepared to advocate for ourselves against electronic voting that can be manipulated without our awareness, against laws that do not protect women from stalkers who use GPS tracking technology, and against images of violence in video games that are created entirely by men. Girls must be equally educated, encouraged, and provided with opportunities in the fields of science and technology. If they aren't, the women of tomorrow won't be able to adequately function in our quickly changing society.

≥ CALL TO ACTION ≤

+ Help your local school district by making sure that there are computers in every classroom, that teachers are using technology to teach their lessons, and that homework assignments include technology. Encourage your employer to donate technology volunteers and computers to the school (see Resources).

+ Ask your local bookstore to put computing or technology magazines in a general section. Too often, these periodicals are placed in a "Men's Interests" section, while the "Women's Interests" section is filled with fashion and cooking magazines. Talk to the bookstore manager about fixing this problem if it exists, or take your business elsewhere.

+ Don't buy video game consoles that don't have adequate games for girls. Write a letter to game companies asking for fewer games geared toward boys alone, and demand that companies get rid of sexist games or games that encourage violence against women (www.women gamers.com).

+ Volunteer your time or donate money to organizations and programs promoting women in science and technology, such as www.digital-sistas.org, www.mentorgirls.org, www.girlstart.org, and www.wgby.org/edu/girlsintech.

+ Ask the girls in your life to help you do Internet research, set up and program the VCR or DVD player, buy your next computer or electronic equipment, and do other technology-related tasks.

+ Provide the girls you know with examples of positive role models; for instance, set up personal meetings or school speaking engagements with women in science and technology (see Resources).

Engage in a New Wave
of Activism

Mia Herndon, Reproductive Health and Justice Program Officer,
Third Wave Foundation

We are ... young women, young men, transgendered individuals, black, Latina, Asian, Middle Eastern, white, biracial, multiracial, all of the above, none of the above, lusciously lesbian, totally hetero, supremely bisexual, absolutely asexual, gloriously gay, none of your business.

We are ... on welfare, comfortable, living check to check, independently wealthy. We believe that violence against women hurts everyone, that foreign policy and drug policy need radical change, that teachers should earn more than CEOs, that education is a right, that the right to choose is fundamental, that prisons hurt families and children, that we need better child care and more affordable housing. We believe that we shouldn't have to choose between our race, class, sexual orientation, and gender; that men can be feminists too; that the traditional binary gender system oppresses both women and men; that art and culture are critical forms of resistance; that war is not an answer to anything.

We are the Third Wave of feminism.

In the early 20th century, everyday women joined together and fought against society and our government to demand their vote in the democratic process. These suffragists, or First Wave feminists, were arrested, imprisoned, and shunned – yet they triumphed.

In the 1970s and 1980s, women around the world joined together in the Second Wave of the women's movement to demand their right to equality on a number of fronts. These women fought in the face of harassment, ridicule, and insurmountable odds. And they made tremendous progress.

Without the efforts of our foremothers, today's young women wouldn't have nearly the opportunities we do. But the work toward social justice is far from complete. All over the country young women are answering the calls of their predecessors and their peers to forge new paths toward equality. In many respects, we're fighting for further progress on the same issues as Second Wave feminism. But we also have our own ideas about how things should be, what issues need to be brought to the table, whom this movement belongs to, and how to address issues that our foremothers struggled with, such as racism and classism.

We use some traditional tactics, and some uniquely our own. We use films, theatre, zines, and funky web technology to organize our activism. We want to create positive social change in innovative and holistic ways, but often we work in isolation or without adequate resources. That's why the Third Wave Foundation was founded: to support and to join forces with other young women's organizations like ours – whose work demands and creates a better today and a brighter tomorrow.

At the Third Wave Foundation, we seek to build partnerships with young activist women and transgendered individuals. We provide financial support nationally to projects that might otherwise be overlooked. Our grants are often the first investment that grantees have received from a national funder or a women's funder, which helps get innovative projects off the ground and open the door to other funding.

As the organizing of our generation continues to grow, we must see an increase in foundation grants to organizations led by young women, as well as an increase in the amount of these grants. With this financial support, we can support new and innovative approaches to pursuing social justice. We can create change in our communities. We can strengthen progressive movements by investing in the next generation of leadership. And we can ensure that young women have the skills, power, and opportunity to engage in and lead these efforts. We need the support of younger and older women alike to make these goals a reality.

≥ CALL TO ACTION ≤

+ Give your time or money to local young women's social justice organizations (see Resources). Ask the organizations you're affiliated with to help support these organizations financially.

+ Learn more about the Third Wave by reading books (see Resources).

+ Take part in the Third Wave Foundation's (www.thirdwavefounda tion.org) many programs, including the "I Spy Sexism" postcard campaign, in which we provide postcards for you to alert your friends, the media, and the culprits themselves about specific incidents of sexism you see in pop culture.

Build the Community You Want to Live In

Create Community Media

Frieda Werden, Cofounder and Producer,
Women's International News Gathering Service

In the mass-media view of our world, men are the authorities on virtually every subject. War is inevitable and even exciting. Buying products and taking designer drugs are the ways to happiness. And women? Why, we're tall and thin with gigantic smiles and few opinions – or else we're not worth any attention.

While we must respond to the mass media's distortion of reality, we can simultaneously spread the word that women come in varied shapes, colors, and opinions – and that this diversity is far more appealing than the vapid alternative. We can showcase the invaluable perspectives of all women, including female (and female-positive) politicians, scholars, activists, and professionals. We can present alternatives to consumerism and help each other become critical thinkers as we confront the destructive messages we're bombarded with daily. And we can make this happen by both supporting and creating alternative media.

In addition to the First Amendment, the Universal Declaration of Human Rights (coauthored by Eleanor Roosevelt and proclaimed in 1948) gives us all the right to be the media. In Article 19, the declaration says, "Everyone has the right to freedom of opinion and expression; this right includes freedom to hold opinions without interference and to seek, receive, and impart information and ideas through any media and regardless of frontiers." Today, in a time when we're too often being told that publicly expressing our opinions is anti-American, we must keep in mind our right and responsibility to speak our educated truths.

First and foremost, it's important for all of us to incorporate some alternative media into our sources of information. This gives us a fuller picture of events and issues. Once you become familiar with the media available, you'll start to have a sense of what stories and perspectives you feel are missing and needed in the mainstream media. And then it's time to take the media into your own hands.

Almost every U.S. community of any size has a community radio station, a public access cable channel, or both, most of which offer free or cheap training. I've been active in community media since 1973, and I've seen how it can effect change throughout the world. Yet sometimes people are reluctant to get involved, because they feel as if nobody's listening. What's important to remember is that even if you only reach 100 listeners, you have the opportunity to change 100 lives and contribute to a ground-swell of positive change.

⋛ CALL TO ACTION ⋜

+ Explore local, national, and global alternative media. A list of U.S. non-commercial radio stations can be found at www.gumbopages.com/other-radio.html. For global community media contacts, visit www.amarc.org. For cable TV access shows, contact your local cable vendor, or look up the Alliance for Community Media at http://www.alliancecm.org.

+ Post your thoughts for the world on a Listserv, a weblog, or your own web page. Indymedia.org offers training and help to upload your work to the Internet.

+ Support the existing alternative media. If you like something, write in or call the station. If the station takes donations, pledge for the shows you want to encourage. Listen to syndicated alternative shows like Democracy Now! (www.democracynow.org), hosted by Amy Goodman, and my program, WINGS (www.wings.org).

+ Use community media to promote your organization or issues. Send press releases and contact shows. Propose yourself as a guest.

+ Contact existing local shows you enjoy, and see if you can volunteer or intern on those shows.

- Start your own show, promote it, and grow the audience. Enlist friends and community members to help schedule guests, do research, choose music, operate a recorder or camera, or even be the face (or voice) of the show.

- Start a radio station. The National Federation of Community Broadcasters (www.nfcb.org) and Prometheus Radio (www.prometheus radio.org) can help.

Put a Stop to Sexual Harassment

Marty Langelan, President, National Woman's Party

What could be more basic than the simple right to walk down a public street? Harassers can make any place a hostile environment: work, school, sports, public parks, even the neighborhood bus stop. They can turn a normal day into an obstacle course of unwelcome comments, propositions, ridicule, racist/sexist/gay-bashing jokes, leering, space invading, humiliation, stalking, sexual extortion, and threats of assault. Harassment is a control mechanism – sometimes subtle, sometimes overt. It can be used to derail careers, coerce sex, or establish "male territory" anywhere, from the boys' tree house to the corporate boardroom.

You probably remember *gender-based harassment* as a kid: "Nyah, nyah, stupid girl." Most of the ten-year-olds in my self-defense classes have also already encountered crude, *explicit sexual harassment* – an often daily experience for women in their teens and 20s, women of color, immigrants, athletes, disabled people, and lesbian/gay/bi/transsexual folks. Many sexual assaults begin with *rape-testing harassment*: a verbal or physical intrusion to test women's reactions and select targets who won't fight back.[1]

The threat of escalation – always just under the surface – is what gives harassment its power. Appeasing or ignoring harassers doesn't work; taking detours to avoid them is no solution; yelling back is dangerous.[2]

What does work? In addition to legal remedies for harassment, we now have an entire "nonviolent confrontation" tool kit, based on 25 years of research and testing, surveys of women around the world, interviews with harassers and rapists, and direct-action workshops with more than 45,000 women and girls. These smart, ethical tactics stop harassers on the spot. Imagine stopping sleazy bosses, creepy professors, lecherous landlords, "Mr. Raincoat" in the park, construction workers hooting and hollering, sexual bullies, gropers, grabbers, street harassers. Imagine no more harassment. We can do it.

+ Consider legal remedies for harassers at work and at school or for officials like landlords or ministers. Document and report the behavior; talk to other women; keep your records in a safe place. If the organization fails to take prompt action, contact a lawyer. Harassment is stressful — ask friends and family for support. Take care of yourself.

+ Use nonviolent confrontation techniques (see my book, *Back Off: How to Confront and Stop Sexual Harassment and Harassers*, and the action steps that follow). Avoid cussing, sarcasm, or insults. Look serious, make eye contact, use a matter-of-fact voice, and be specific.

+ Address street harassment with this simple, all-purpose statement: "Stop harassing women. I don't like it — no one likes it. Show some respect." Most harassers fold instantly.

+ With people you know, try the A-B-C Statement, or write an A-B-C Letter: When you do A, the effect is B; I want C from now on. "When you stare at women's breasts, it's conspicuous and embarrassing to everyone in the room. We want you to look us in the face from now on."

+ Set a firm, immediate boundary by naming the behavior: Say out loud exactly what the harasser is doing. Be brief, clear, and direct as you state the behavior, the principle, and the command: "You are exposing yourself. This is about respect. Put that penis back in your pants right now." If the harasser makes excuses, hold him accountable: "You heard me. Show some respect."

+ Interrupt everyday harassment with the Socratic Question: very seriously, ask the harasser to explain exactly what he/she just said or did. "Can you explain why you call women 'sweetie'?" The more ridiculous the behavior, the more impossible it is to explain.

+ Use group action to confront persistent harassers. At neighborhood sessions, we trained 250 subway riders to say just one line whenever they saw their local harasser: "Stop harassing women." They did. He's gone.

+ Give men the chance to be allies by asking them to tell a harasser that *they* don't like what he's doing. And be a cross-boundary ally yourself. Sometimes it's easier to take action when you're not the target. You may have more safety or job security than those who are being harassed. Speak up. If you're white, interrupt racist jokes. If you're straight, challenge gay bashing. Speak on your own account: say that *you* don't want to hear it. That ten-second technique makes all the difference in the world.

Eradicate Racism

Mal Johnson, Cochair, National Women's Conference, and
C. DeLores Tucker, Founder, National Congress of Black Women

Forty years ago, in March 1965, the two of us marched arm in arm
with 25,000 black Southerners and liberal white Northerners
across the Edmund Pettus Bridge in Selma, Alabama, to protest the denial
of voting rights for American citizens of color. We were motivated by the
words of Dr. Martin Luther King, Jr., who expressed his dream for all of
us at the historic March on Washington, where he called for a nation
whose races all lived in harmony. After both those marches, we went
home to Philadelphia, a city where racism was subtler than in the South
but just as pervasive. We grew up in a community that was rapidly
devolving from segregated black and white neighborhoods and schools
to all-black ghettoes. We witnessed the rise in crime, the economic depri-
vation, and the alienation of the younger generation.

We knew that education and leadership training would be our way to
create change. Mal is still emotional as she recalls the prestigious job she
landed as a radio and television correspondent in a Washington, D.C.-
based news bureau – she wasn't hired because she was fully qualified,
but because the station needed a "black face" in the aftermath of the 1964
Civil Rights Act. For the 27 years she remained in that job, no other
African American reporter was ever hired. DeLores decided it was time
for black people to move into politics, and she bravely sought elected
office. We mounted a vigorous campaign toward that end, and in 1968
she became the first African American secretary of state in Pennsylvania. No other black woman has since served in that office.

Since the civil rights movement, women of color have organized on
many fronts. The largest coalition of women's organizations in America,
the National Council of Women's Organizations, includes 14 organizations devoted to advancing women of color and to advocating public policies for all women. In addition, a number of traditionally white women's

organizations are headed and staffed by women of color. While tensions have always existed between predominantly white women's organizations and organizations for women of color, the movements to combat sexism and racism have moved closer together over the years, and today they collaborate on common concerns.

Women of color have also been making advances in education. In 1999 to 2000, African Americans made up 12 percent of college students; Hispanic or Latinos, 11 percent; and Asian Americans, 5 percent; and more than half of each group were women students! Notably, 300,000 African American women hold master's degrees, and more than 6,000 have earned doctorates. Women of color have also made strides in the workplace. According to the 2000 Census, 41 percent of Asian American women, 30 percent of African American and Native American women, and 23 percent of Hispanic or Latina women were employed in managerial or professional occupations in 2000, compared to 39 percent of white women. Women of color are joining professions in the legal, medical, religious, and scientific fields, yet the majority of these women work in technical, sales, and administrative support jobs. Many women of color are still employed in the lower-paying service sector, earning a living as domestic servants or child care providers.

No single group of women of color can claim adequate representation in corporate America or in the body politic. Racism still rears its ugly head for women of color, sometimes on a daily basis and many times subtly. For example, women of color are often overlooked for senior promotions because of our society's unspoken aversion to having women of color supervise white employees. Vacant houses or apartments suddenly become unavailable when landlords discover that the would-be renter is a woman of color. And women of color anecdotally report being followed by security and getting the brush-off from sales people in department stores. While 13 women of color serve as members of Congress, they represent only 3 percent of all the elected representatives in Congress.

At its best, the United States is a vibrant country that owes its open-mindedness and generosity of spirit to a wealth of multicultural experiences. Today, the American population is becoming more diverse than ever before. By 2050, it's estimated that half of all American women will be women of color. The changing demographic of the nation may reduce racism, but not necessarily. African nations with white minorities in power have perpetuated systems of discrimination, such as apartheid, for decades, and a legacy of racism remains. American women and men will need to work hard to eradicate racism even in the face of an increasingly diverse society.

Issues of color affect all people everywhere, for they are issues of basic human rights. The pursuit of equality for women of color is a work in progress that requires women and men to work together, with people of all races sharing wisdom and providing mutual support. We must start by examining our daily thoughts and actions to reach out across color barriers.

⋛ CALL TO ACTION ⋚

+ Examine social movements to determine how they can aid in the struggle to eradicate racism.

+ Share experiences of racism with girls, young adults, and other women.

+ Teach children at an early age to respect all people, avoid racial slurs, and stand up to discrimination

+ Participate in political campaigns to become knowledgeable about the candidate's degree of interest in abolishing racism.

+ Join a professional or emotionally supportive organization that provides a web of peers, mentors, or resources. (See Resource Section)

+ Report acts of racism in the workplace and demand response/action.

+ Abandon the emotional energy required to sustain anger caused about acts of racism and replace that energy with efforts to address racist acts.

Insist on Equal Rights
for Lesbians

. . . .

Patricia Ireland, Advisory Board Member, Gender Public Advocacy Coalition

In 1976, a commissioner of Florida's Miami-Dade County, Ruth Shack, put herself in the eye of a political storm when she sponsored one of the nation's first ordinances banning discrimination based on sexual orientation. In January 1977, a divided commission passed the ordinance, and a vicious campaign to repeal it began.

Six months later, voters repealed the ordinance by a lopsided 208,504 to 92,212. Concerned by the vote and inspired by Commissioner Shack, I volunteered in her 1978 reelection effort — my first venture into electoral politics. Commissioner Shack won reelection, but the campaign was brutal.

We've made great progress since then. Eighty-five percent of people polled say lesbians and gay men should have equal employment opportunity.[3] Sexual-orientation discrimination is illegal in more than a dozen states and hundreds of municipalities.[4] But progress does not mean equality. Why are equal rights, especially equal marriage rights, still hot-button issues?

Working toward lesbian rights means challenging deeply held beliefs about women and men. This creates conflict and makes people, at best, uncomfortable. Also, using the tension generated by these issues remains an effective political tactic against those who advocate equality.

Women activists have long found our sexuality challenged. Newspapers described participants in the first-ever women's rights conference in 1848 in Seneca Falls, New York, as "mannish" and pointedly described Susan B. Anthony as a "spinster." The vote for women was deemed "unnatural." The implication was clear, and some women withdrew support from women's suffrage to avoid being seen as lesbians.

This scare tactic provides both principled reasons to fight for lesbian rights and a pragmatic reason to do so: currently, the fear of being identified as a lesbian is used to intimidate women and drive us back from our pursuit of equality – and from each other. Every woman who speaks up and speaks out, who is confident, competent, and ambitious, or seeks a nontraditional role is likely to be tagged a lesbian. Until the time when being identified as a lesbian, whether true or not, no longer means a woman could lose her job, custody of her children, or even her life, those threatened by our progress will continue to use this tactic to divide and weaken us.

To achieve civil rights for lesbians and for all women, we must challenge the narrow gender stereotypes that perpetuate discrimination based on both sex and sexual orientation. Gender stereotypes are strict expectations that society maintains for each sex: how we are expected to walk, talk, and look; what we're told to wear and what kind of work we're encouraged to do; whom we're supposed to love and form families with. All women are limited to some extent by these rigid expectations, whether you're a woman who wants to be a welder rather than a waitress, a girl who plays ice hockey instead of figure skating, or a woman who loves women rather than (or in addition to) men. You can help pick up the pace of progress.

≥ CALL TO ACTION ≤

+ Learn more about gender and lesbian rights so you'll be comfortable discussing the issues. Gender PAC (www.gpac.org) and the Human Rights Campaign (www.hrc.org) are good places to start.

+ Write letters to the editor responding to stereotypical assumptions about women or biased comments about lesbians.

+ Raise the issue of lesbian rights in public forums with elected officials and candidates. Congress members and state officials can be found through http://thomas.loc.gov.

+ Sign up for email alerts to stay updated on issues, so you can call legislators and local media outlets to voice your opinion. One place to

---

sign up is the website of the National Lesbian and Gay Task Force (www.thetaskforce.org).

+ Speak up when someone demeans lesbians or women who are not in traditional roles. Brainstorm with friends in advance about responses that will invite dialogue, not defensiveness.

+ Build bridges between lesbians and straight women. One way is to support women's groups that actively pursue lesbian rights as part of their agendas. The National Organization for Women (www.now. org), for example, advocates for all women. The Gay, Lesbian, and Straight Education Alliance (www.glsen.org) is another good resource.

Value Diversity and Promote Cultural Understanding

Kiran Ahuja, National Director,

National Asian Pacific American Women's Forum

I grew up starved for racial and cultural diversity. In Savannah, Georgia, I was one of few South Asians in my school. My brother and I struggled with being the only kids with olive skin, dark eyes, a small frame, and a mother who wore traditional garb. We tolerated insensitive comments and stares. And then, partly because of these experiences, my brother succumbed to the pressures of his life by committing suicide when he was 25. He was not alone: Asian Pacific Americans between the ages of 15 and 24 have one of the highest suicide rates in this country. Experts suggest that cultural norms and traditional family pressures in a Western society may contribute to this high rate of suicide.

The experience my brother and I shared is no different from that of the many young immigrants who are growing up in emerging immigrant communities across this country. When these young people and their families are not in a culturally-tolerant environment, they are often subject to extreme social pressures and discrimination. Consistently, we see that a diverse school, neighborhood, and workplace foster tolerance and acceptance of different cultures through exposure to other groups, shared stories, and a raised consciousness. Where racial diversity is hard to achieve, schools and communities must become sensitized to the needs of immigrant populations and people of color, and they must actively promote cultural understanding – for the benefit of everyone in the community. Emphasizing multicultural education, affirmative action programs, heritage months, and ethnic and women's studies in colleges is an example of how we can value diversity.

Though Latinos and African Americans are "majority-minority" communities and Asian Pacific Americans are the fastest-growing minority, our government, companies, organizations, television shows, and segregated neighborhoods do not reflect this diversity in American culture, nor do these entities send the message that appreciation of diversity is a noble goal.

Race has a history of dividing our country, but the advancements that have been hard won by civil rights activists over the past 50 years promised a more equal and united future. Unfortunately, legal attacks against diversity-promoting programs like affirmative action are setting us back decades. Today, our schools are more segregated than before the Supreme Court's landmark Brown vs. the Board of Education decision.[5] If, as a society, we do not choose to value and support diversity, stories like my brother's will multiply. The current cultural and legal trend is perpetuating segregation, isolation among communities, and eventually strife.

As head of an Asian Pacific American women's rights organization, I understand that achieving diversity within the women's movement is a high priority as well. We, as women of all races and ethnicities, can set an example for the rest of the country – we can show how to give immigrant women and women of color due regard for their contributions and struggles and due place in organizations, institutions, and governments. As women, we understand the consequences of being undervalued and discriminated against because of our gender. Together we must actively pursue an appreciation for diversity in our own communities. And we must realize that we cannot ask for something that is not reflected in our own movement.

≳ CALL TO ACTION ≲

+ Vote for and support the campaigns of minority female candidates, with a progressive agenda who are sorely under-represented in our government.

+ Support and promote multicultural and bilingual education in schools by approaching principals, administrators, and school board members about these programs. Encourage your child's teacher to invite visitors of different nationalities to share their stories with the

---

classroom. Share with your children your own experiences traveling, meeting foreign visitors, and maintaining diverse friendships, and discuss how these experiences are enriching.

+ Actively support affirmative action and other programs that promote diversity in schools, on college campuses, and in workplaces.

+ Encourage local companies and television shows to diversify their workforce and actors/crew, respectively. You can do this by writing or calling or by joining forces with media advocacy groups. For example, the National Asian Pacific American Legal Consortium (www. napalc.org) is working to persuade media networks to diversify the industry.

+ Create a more diverse women's movement by supporting organizations run by emerging women of color with your time and your money (see Resources).

Mandate Responsible Gun Policy

Mary Leigh Blek, President Emeritus, Million Mom March

I used to think my family was immune from gun violence. That is, until June 29, 1994, when my 21-year-old son, Matthew, was shot and killed during an attempted robbery by teenagers wielding a Saturday Night Special handgun. So many dreams and hopes for a bright future died that day.

Sadly, my family is not alone in our suffering. In 2001, almost 30,000 Americans died from gunshot wounds. Guns are the second-leading cause of death (after motor vehicle accidents) for our young people. The toll of more than 80 gun deaths each day in America is unacceptable.[6]

While the underlying causes of violence need to be addressed, we must also address the lethality that guns bring to this violence. Our firearm death rate for children under 15 is 12 times higher than the rate for 25 other industrialized nations combined.[7] We must have policies that mandate responsibility and accountability in the way guns are designed, manufactured, marketed, distributed, and used in our society. We do this for cars and drivers, why not for firearms?

Polls indicate that the majority of Americans support strong gun laws. Unfortunately, misinformation and a powerful gun lobby keep our government from adequately regulating firearms and protecting our families. For instance, the Consumer Product Safety Commission is prohibited from addressing gun safety; federal law does not limit the number of handguns someone can purchase in a given period of time; and unregulated sales at gun shows allow unlicensed dealers to sell guns with no questions asked.

We need to educate and mobilize our fellow citizens into action in order to stop gun violence. One way we can do this is by sharing well-respected research. For example, the risk of homicide in the home is 3 times greater in households with guns than in those without, and the risk of suicide is 5 times greater; a gun in the home is 22 times more likely to be used in a homicide, suicide, or unintentional shooting than to kill in self-defense.[8]

We must also demand that gun owners are informed about safe storage practices, such as keeping the gun and ammunition separate and both securely locked. Local ordinances must require guns to be sold in secure storefronts and not at residential "kitchen tables." And state laws need to require domestic violence offenders to relinquish guns in order to reduce the risk to a battered spouse.

At the Brady Campaign to Prevent Gun Violence united with the Million Mom March, we are working toward all of these changes, in addition to reinstating the ten-year-old federal assault weapon ban that Congress allowed to expire in September 2004. The ban resulted in a reduction of gun crimes using assault weapons by 66 percent.[9] We don't need to be reminded what an assault weapon with a large-capacity magazine can do in a school yard full of children. We remember Stockton, California, and Columbine High School in Colorado.

As a public health nurse, I am proud of everyone who is working to address the epidemic of gun violence. Safety shouldn't be a partisan issue. However, the gun lobby has turned gun violence into a political battle. This leaves us no choice but to participate in the political arena in order to save the lives of ourselves and our loved ones.

⋛ **CALL TO ACTION** ⋜

+ Speak out! When you hear about a shooting, express your thoughts and feelings to loved ones and to the organizations you belong to, including faith-based organizations. Give them resources so they can take action to prevent gun violence.

+ With your time and money, support national organizations working to prevent gun violence, such as the Brady Campaign to Prevent Gun Violence (www.bradycampaign.org), the Million Mom March (www.million mommarch.org), and the Coalition to Stop Gun Violence (www.csgv.org).

- ✦ Sign up for an email action list to add your voice of support to national or state gun control issues (www.stategunlaws.org, www.Stop theNRA.com, www.csgv.org).

- ✦ Write letters to editors, policymakers, and elected officials at the local, state, and national levels (find your officials at www.bradycampaign.org) to express your viewpoints on the issues and proposed legislation.

- ✦ Remember to thank those who support your views, and vote for candidates who advocate responsible gun policies.

Support Labor Unions

Pamela Wilson, Assistant to the President,
Department for Professional Employees, AFL-CIO

Big Business in America has never made much effort to hide its contempt for (and fear of) labor unions. For more than a century, U.S. corporations and industries have wielded considerable legal, economic, and sometimes literal weapons against unionized workers. What you may not know is that increasing numbers of professional and other women are forming and joining unions today and unions are amplifying their voices, improving their conditions, and changing their lives.

Arlene Chester's union (AFSCME Local 626) won the first class action lawsuit filed under the Congressional Accountability Act and ended decades of discrimination against the women who clean Congressional offices. The victory brought Arlene and her 300 coworkers pay raises, pension adjustments, and back-pay lump sums.

Navidad Dullas, a registered nurse at San Francisco's Laguna Honda Hospital, reports that her union (SEIU Local 790) is helping the community by battling the government when it abandons its commitment to public health. Her union gives her a voice to solve conflicts, and it helps improve patient care. Navidad says: "With the union, we have a say in the administration."

Through joining with others in a union, women can gain better wages and benefits, more respect on the job, a means to counterbalance the otherwise unchecked power of employers, a voice in improving the quality of the specialized services they provide and of the products they produce, and more flexibility for work and family responsibilities.

More than 6.7 million working women belong to labor unions, and women currently account for 44 percent of all union members, up from 19 percent in 1962.[10] Women are forming and joining unions at a faster rate than men: 55 percent of all newly organized workers are women.[11]

The wage gap between women and men remains a serious and pervasive problem for professional women and for women in every occupational category. Union representation is a proven and powerful means for raising wages, especially for those most subject to labor market discrimination, such as women and minorities. In 2003, union women earned weekly wages that were 33 percent higher than those of nonunion women, while union men earned 21 percent more than nonunion men. Earnings for African American, Latina, and Asian women who were union members exceeded those of their nonunion counterparts by 36, 49, and 21 percent, respectively.[12] Higher union wages for women translate into a better standard of living for U.S. families, stronger tax bases for our communities, better schools and infrastructures, and healthier local economies.

Besides an increase in wages, unions also improve women's lives by providing greater access to employer-sponsored benefits. Forty-five million Americans – many of them employed women – lack health insurance. Unionized women and men are far more likely to have employer-provided health insurance, and among the insured, union members receive more generous health benefits. Fifty-one percent of union members have dental coverage and 37 percent have vision coverage, versus 30 and 17 percent, respectively, for nonunion workers. Union members also pay lower health deductibles and a smaller share of the costs for family coverage. They are also 14 percent more likely to have life insurance and 33 percent more likely to have disability insurance.[13, 14]

Retirement security is another key issue. Not only do union women receive better pay and therefore larger Social Security checks, but they are far more likely to receive a pension. Seventy-four percent of union members have guaranteed (defined-benefit) pension plans, versus 15 percent of nonunion workers. In addition, employers of unionized workers contribute 28 percent more toward employee pensions. Union members also receive more vacation time and more total paid leave than their nonunion counterparts.[15]

Now more than 50 percent white-collar and 44 percent female, unions are being transformed by the changes in their composition. Union policies increasingly reflect women's concerns, prompting major efforts to guarantee an end to occupational and salary discrimination and to bring about increased child care assistance and parental leave, flexible work schedules, greater opportunities for education and training, an end to sexual harassment and violence against women, equity in Social Security, and pension and insurance reform that ends any gender bias. Through women's committees and departments in their unions, and through the Coalition for Labor Union Women (CLUW) – the only national organization specifically for union women – women are working within the labor movement to advance their agenda.

Unions support women, amplifying their voices and making them heard. Through collective bargaining, women can improve the quality of their work, something of key importance to the increasing numbers of women in professional and technical occupations. Through unions, nurses have achieved higher standards for patient care, teachers have created opportunities for better classroom instruction, and social workers have successfully limited caseloads at human service agencies to ensure better care. There are many such examples. And because of those, it's no stretch to say that union membership changes women's lives.

⇒ CALL TO ACTION ⇐

+ Join a union — if you're not already part of the union movement, you should be, regardless of your walk of life. Working women in all walks of life come together in unions to have a voice at work. In fact, there are more union members among professionals than any other occupational group. Visit the websites of organizations such as the AFL-CIO (www.aflcio.org), the Coalition of Labor Union Women (www.cluw.org), and the Department for Professional Employees, AFL-CIO (www.dpeaflcio.org) to learn more about unions, and specifically about women and unions. Connect with your local union movement.

+ If you are a union member, be an active one. Participate in your union. Participate in CLUW.

+ Support organizing efforts in your community. Don't just drive by picket lines and labor rallies — get involved. Unions lift up communities by raising the standard of living.

+ Join the Working Families e-Activist Network (www.unionvoice.org/wfean/join.html) for occasional action alerts, to find out when your voice is needed for online actions with offline impact.

Reach for
the World

Uphold Women's Rights
as Human Rights

Sarah Albert, Public Policy Director,
The General Federation of Women's Clubs

Most women in developing societies struggle daily in the face of violence, poverty, lack of legal status, and the inability to be civically active. The statistics of women around the world are staggering: One in three women are abused during their lifetimes.[1] Two-thirds of the world's 799 million illiterate adults are women.[2] Yearly, two million girls between ages 5 and 15 are sold into sexual slavery.[3] More than 500,000 women die annually from pregnancy-related complications.[4] Women, more vulnerable than men to contract HIV/AIDS, have substantially higher infection rates.[5]

To address these problems, more than 90 percent of the United Nations member states have ratified a human rights treaty known as the Treaty for the Rights of Women, formerly known as the UN Convention on the Elimination of All Forms of Discrimination Against Women (CEDAW). CEDAW is regarded as the most important international mechanism for women's equality. It addresses physical, sexual, economic, and political abuses against women and promotes women's equality of rights and well-being. This treaty holds that basic human rights for women should be universal across cultures and religions.

CEDAW's provisions are consistent with U.S. law and include rights that many American women take for granted, such as access to education, legal redress against domestic violence, and access to health care. Yet the United States has not ratified the Treaty for the Rights of Women.

Not ratifying CEDAW has dampened our country's leadership in promoting human rights, democracy, and the rule of law. During Senate hearings in 2002, Yale law professor Harold Hongju Koh noted, "Lack of U.S. ratification has hindered our role as a human rights leader, damaged our diplomatic relations, and reduced our international standing."[6]

Our country has a bipartisan tradition of supporting international standards through treaties, but efforts to ratify CEDAW have failed due to lack of political will. There is no reason for the United States not to ratify this treaty. Its principles are longtime mainstays of U.S. law and custom.

In its 25-plus years of existence, CEDAW has provided an opportunity for ratifying countries to overcome barriers of discrimination. Similar to other human rights treaties, it sets basic human rights standards but does not impose laws. Participating countries are required to examine and report on conditions for women and girls.

The treaty established a monitoring system, the CEDAW Committee, which reviews and keeps track of the progress of member states. Though the treaty provisions are nonbinding, this monitoring process has proven valuable in enforcing the scope and spirit of the treaty by advancing social and political awareness.

CEDAW has been used to incorporate women's rights into national constitutions, eliminate discriminatory laws, and influence court decisions. Measures have been taken against sex slavery, domestic violence, and the trafficking of women. Women's health care services have improved, saving lives during pregnancy and childbirth. Millions of women have secured loans and gained the right to own and inherit property.

For example, the Ukraine, Nepal, Thailand, and the Philippines passed laws to stop the trafficking of women and girls for forced prostitution. India developed guidelines on preventing sexual assault. Nicaragua, Jordan, and Egypt significantly increased literacy rates after improving access to education for girls and women. Colombia outlawed domestic violence and established legal protection for its victims. Australia and Luxembourg launched health campaigns promoting the awareness and prevention of breast and cervical cancers.

There is much more improvement to be made. U.S. failure to ratify the treaty allows countries with weak human rights records to neglect and undermine human rights for women. Until the United States ratifies CEDAW, our country cannot credibly demand that others live up to their obligations under the treaty. U.S. ratificatin of CEDAW is long overdue.

⟩ CALL TO ACTION ⟨

+ Learn more about the Treaty for the Rights of Women at www.womens treaty.org.

+ Call and write the president and your senators to support U.S. ratification of this treaty.

+ Write a letter to the editor of your local newspaper about CEDAW.

+ Initiate and support the passage of local and state resolutions calling for U.S. ratification of CEDAW. For more information about how to do so, visit www.womenstreaty.org.

Address the Unique Needs of Immigrant Women

Hilda L. Solis, U.S. Representative

Immigrant women in the United States are incredibly diverse in many ways: their socioeconomic status, country of origin, educational background, traditional cultural beliefs, and legal status. Yet many face common challenges that differ from those facing United States–born women and male immigrants. Three pressing issues that impact immigrant women in unique ways are domestic violence within immigrant families, workers' rights, and access to education.

Domestic violence impacts women in all demographics. Yet confusion about legal protections under immigration laws, lack of economic independence, and the shortage of culturally and linguistically appropriate resources are obstacles facing many battered immigrant women. In addition, one study focusing on undocumented Latina immigrants shows that a primary barrier to these women seeking help from social service agencies is the fear of deportation. Even if immigrant women seek to press charges against their abusers, most courts don't have translators to facilitate communication between these women and court officials.

Immigrant women face similar barriers to achieving full and just workers' rights. Approximately 14 percent of the civilian labor force are immigrants, who fulfill critical jobs yet they are disproportionately forced into lower-wage industries such as the garment, domestic, and hotel sectors. In addition, they are often subjected to poor working conditions, earn less than minimum wage, and suffer discrimination and exploitation in the workplace. Immigrant women often feel too scared about legal or immigration status to seek help or escape. As a result, immigrant women are often unable to achieve economic self-sufficiency, and they must struggle to provide for their children and families.

One crucial step toward empowering immigrant women is to provide them with access to education. Common obstacles often result in low enrollment and high dropout rates, whether we are talking about immigrant youth who arrive in the U.S. school system with significant gaps in their schooling or older immigrant women with limited proficiency in English who are looking to continue their education. Bilingual education programs, Pell grants and other financial assistance, and improved access to higher education for undocumented immigrants are all critical in securing educational and employment opportunities for immigrant women. In an effort to improve access to our nation's job training system, I introduced legislation (H.R. 1992) to reduce the barriers to job training for those with limited English proficiency; this legislation creates incentives to develop programs that integrate job training with language acquisition and civics courses.

Immigrant women have made, and continue to make, incredible strides and unique contributions to our nation's families and communities. However, as community members, policymakers, educators, and advocates, we must actively work to ensure the health and well-being of immigrant women and give them the tools to take action as well.

⋛ CALL TO ACTION ⋚

+ Ask your representative to support legislation such as the Domestic Violence Prevention, Education, and Awareness Act (H.R.3425), which I introduced to help develop culturally sensitive and multilingual media campaigns about domestic violence for underserved minority and immigrant communities.

+ Express similar support for the Domestic Violence Courts Assistance Act (H.R.3424), which I introduced to provide grants so that municipal court systems could set up specialized domestic violence courts; such courts would speed up the legal process and increase conviction rates for all cases. The law would also help to pay for translators in the courts.

- Urge your representative to cosponsor the Safe, Orderly, Legal Visas and Enforcement (SOLVE) Act (H.R.4262), introduced by Rep. Luis Gutierrez, which would provide an earned adjustment to legal status for America's hardworking, taxpaying undocumented immigrant workers who play by the rules. It would also expand legal opportunities for workers who come to fill our labor needs in the future, as well as reduce the backlog in the family immigration system.

- Urge your representative to support the Student Adjustment Act/Development, Relief, and Education for Alien Minors (DREAM) Act (H.R. 1684/S. 1545), which would allow states to determine a student's eligibility for resident status for tuition and admissions purposes and would also help students of good standing gain resident status so that they can apply for jobs.

Combat Human Trafficking

Melanne Verveer, Chair, Vital Voices Global Partnership

Each year, at least one million human beings, predominantly women, are shipped across national boundaries and sold into what has become modern-day slavery. No country is immune from this problem. Approximately 15,000 people are trafficked into the United States each year.[7] No country can eradicate trafficking by itself because the problem is international in scope. With victims moving between countries and through countries, progress is only possible through transnational cooperation among government and nongovernment agencies.

Human trafficking is one of the most profound violations of human rights. It is a pressing global law enforcement challenge, a growing health problem because of the HIV/AIDS pandemic, and a national security concern.

People who are trafficked are desperate for economic opportunity. They think they are applying for jobs as waitresses, laborers, entertainers, or child care providers, only to find themselves in an unimaginable nightmare living in captivity. They are brutalized into sexual exploitation, domestic servitude, or sweatshops. Enticed through false advertising and deceptive offers, they fall prey to organized criminal networks.

The trafficking of human beings is a flourishing criminal industry, generating billions of dollars every year. Interpol, the international police organization, has called it the fastest-growing crime in the world. Routes used to ship illegal drugs and arms are being used at this very moment to ship human beings. Traffickers derive enormous profits from their sales because of the relatively low risk of prosecution, partly due to the fact that their work is often facilitated by corrupt politicians. In some countries, selling human beings is less risky than selling drugs.

Trafficking has exploded in recent years because of a combination of factors. The criminal networks are highly organized and growing, and they've developed local operatives that prey on vulnerable people who are trapped in poverty. Many places that were once closed societies have newly opened borders, and the criminal traffickers have taken advantage of this new freedom of movement. Information technology and the ease of transportation have also had a hand in facilitating criminal operations. Coupled with the increasing demand for cheap labor, as well as the increasing demand in countries with a large sex industry, these conditions are creating a fast-growing epidemic.

It is critical for countries to pass strong laws to protect the victims and to crack down on the perpetrators. In the United States, the Trafficking Victims Protection Act was signed into law in 2000 and reauthorized in 2003. It is a very important tool, one that can serve as a model for other countries, to confront the traffickers and assist the victims.

To prevent this crime from growing, we must enhance public awareness of it and develop education campaigns to alert women and girls in urban and rural areas alike of the threat. Above all, the best prevention program is access to economic opportunity.

Stiff new criminal statutes and penalties are making the prosecution of the perpetrators possible, especially where the laws enable victims to stay in the country and help the prosecution.

In the United States, there is still work to be done. We need to allocate more resources for training and equipping law enforcement to deal with these crimes. We need to improve our prosecution record. And we need to work with other countries to enable them to combat trafficking more effectively. In addition, the Senate should ratify the Protocol to Prevent, Suppress, and Punish Trafficking in Persons. This is an international instrument that the United States helped negotiate, under which countries obligate themselves to enact laws against trafficking.

⋛ CALL TO ACTION ⋜

+ Contact your U.S. senators and urge them to ratify and implement the Protocol to Prevent, Suppress, and Punish Trafficking in Persons, Especially Women and Children. This protocol supplements the UN Convention Against Transnational Organized Crime.

- Encourage your state representatives and senators to pass anti-trafficking legislation based on the federal statute.

- Invite speakers to address this issue in your community in order to raise public awareness. Vital Voices (www.vitalvoices.org) provides tool kits, fliers, and resources for finding speakers.

- Sign up for the Trafficking Alert newsletter to stay informed on local and global news www.vitalvoices.org/programs/anti-trafficking/trafficking_alert.

Wage Peace around the World

Swanee Hunt, Founder, Women Waging Peace

Even though women around the globe play a vital role in averting violence and resolving conflict, their work in the field of security is largely unrecognized at the institutional and public policy levels. With expertise in grassroots activism, political leadership, investigative journalism, human rights law, military reform, negotiations, and postconflict reconstruction, women are bringing effective innovations to the security process.

Women Waging Peace was developed in 1999 to bridge the gap between women's work for lasting peace and the decisions being made in the public policy arena. Our organization advocates for the full participation of women in formal and informal peace processes, and urges networking and collaboration to promote sustainable peace.

"Sustainable" is the key word, since conflict is cyclical in nature. Without stabilization, the postconflict period quickly becomes a preconflict state, and war flares up again. Afghanistan, for example, currently exhibits an extreme fragility that can easily evolve into full-scale violence. Against a historical backdrop of foreign invasion and religious extremism, warlords and militia are still prevalent. The constitutional Loya Jirga, or national assembly, has built a solid framework for a new society, but it rests on the shifting sands of dramatic changes in leadership and law. Although the new constitution for Afghanistan has been written, the country's need for aid and support cannot be written off.

An important piece of reconstruction is elevating the status of women. Without education, women will not be able to partake in the opportunities that the international community is helping to ensure.

Afghani women have shown extraordinary courage as they have raised their own and others' voices. Sakena Yakoobi ran underground schools under the Taliban, eventually founding the Afghan Institute for Learning, which offers workshops on human rights and leadership. Rina

Amiri, a refugee, left the security of the United States to work for the United Nations within Afghanistan, training women to run for office and organizing polling places for the Loya Jirga.

In 1998, during the Taliban rule, I visited Afghan refugee camps inside neighboring Pakistan. In a two-room home serving as a clandestine school, I found 25 Afghan girls and women sitting on the mud floor, learning to read; they started by identifying their names on squares of paper spread out in the center of the room. I asked a middle-aged woman her motivation. She smiled slyly. "I want to know if our local mullah is telling the truth about what the Koran requires of women."

Peace building is more than compelling warring parties to lower their weapons and stop the bullets from flying. True peace means creating a safe and stable society. Unlike traditional concepts of national security, which focus almost exclusively on a state and military balance of power, "human security" includes human rights, protection from dangers, and empowerment of people to participate in decision making. Some issues that negatively impact human security, often with a disproportionate effect on women, include:

+ Lack of education, especially for girls
+ Impunity for war criminals and other perpetrators
+ Infectious diseases, including HIV/AIDS, and poor health care
+ Poverty and neglect of basic needs like water and shelter
+ Trafficking in persons, especially sex trade with women and children
+ Proliferation of small arms throughout society
+ Violence against women
+ Denial of political rights

At any given time, some 40 countries around the world are in conflict. Over 17 million people have been forced from their homes. These problems require action, not only by national governments and the UN but also by millions of individuals.

+ Donate money, time, and supplies to the Afghan Institute of Learning (www.creatinghope.org/ail.htm). Before throwing away a duplicate stapler or the box of crayons children have outgrown, collect them and ask neighbors, friends, and coworkers to add items to the box. AIL can use office and medical supplies, from pens to LCD projectors, from vitamins to disposable syringes.

+ Consider teaching in Kabul and other postconflict nations. Visit TeachAbroad.com or VolunteerAbroad.com to search for job and volunteer opportunities around the globe.

+ Contact members of Congress who serve on committees that address foreign and defense policies to urge them to support reconstruction programs that improve human security, strengthen rule of law, and promote women's rights (see Resources).

+ Volunteer with or donate to nongovernmental organizations (NGOs), such as Amnesty International (www.amnesty.org) or Save the Children (www.savethechildren.org).

Impact Foreign Policy

June Zeitlin, Executive Director,
Women's Environment and Development Organization

Increasingly, American women are broadening their political awareness and action to address foreign policy issues. We're seeing the connections between national issues and global policy. And we understand that we live in an interdependent world where this country's foreign policy greatly impacts women and families at home and abroad.

More and more U.S. resources are devoted to war and militarism abroad – at the expense of social programs at home. The U.S. government is also working to repeal measures to protect women's rights. For example, at the UN, the U.S. administration has openly reversed its long-standing support for the 1994 Beijing Platform for Action and the 1995 Cairo Programme of Action, the most comprehensive international commitments guaranteeing women's rights.[8] Also, Congress has pressed to include a conditionality clause with respect to development cooperation funds, aimed to prevent organizations that are in any way connected with pregnancy termination from accessing such funds.[9] According to a recent report by the International Working Group on Sexuality and Social Policy, "Since President Bush came into power, the White House has adopted a host of policies and rules and reinforced existing measures that have systematically attacked human rights in matters of sexuality, at home and abroad."[10]

But we are not powerless against these regressive policies. As conservative forces step up their efforts to roll back women's rights, we can find innovative and successful ways to fight back. The Women's Environment and Development Organization (WEDO) and its partnering organizations published a series of "global scorecards" (www.wglobalscorecard. org) throughout 2003 and 2004 grading the U.S. government's rhetoric on women compared to the reality of its impacts on women's day-to-day lives across the globe.

In 2002, the U.S. administration decided to withhold funds for the

United Nations Family Planning Fund; in response, two local women started 34 Million Friends of UNFPA, which has raised more than $2 million in donations. CODEPINK, an organization of women taking a stand for peace, fired up women to act locally against the invasion in Iraq; women activists dressed in attention-grabbing bright pink and participated in the massive antiwar demonstrations of 2003 and 2004. WILD for Human Rights spearheaded the passage of a San Francisco city ordinance to the Convention on the Elimination of All Forms of Discrimination Against Women (CEDAW). The U.S. Congress, meanwhile, still refuses to ratify this 1979 international bill of rights for women, along with a handful of such "rogue" states as Iran, Somalia, Syria, and Sudan.

U.S. women and their male allies can and must advocate for a U.S. foreign policy that advances international law and human rights, including women's rights, and strengthens the role of the United Nations. In order for the United States to develop a foreign policy that reflects a peaceful and just vision of U.S. global engagement, as well as human rights for women around the world, it is essential that U.S. women raise their voices and take concrete actions toward change.

⇒ CALL TO ACTION ⇐

+ Get the facts. Find out the U.S. position on key international treaties and their effects on women around the world and in the United States at www.undaw.org.

+ Connect with women around the world working for equality in global policy (see Resources). Help to plan actions at home or support them abroad.

+ Spread the word. Use the facts to sensitize women in your area and get them involved. Organizing together can broaden your outreach. For example, you can host regular gatherings with the women in your community to write letters to the local media, plan group visits to your elected officials to lobby for the issues you support, and develop and circulate flyers to raise awareness of specific legislation or conditions. If possible, name your group and create a website to encourage new members.

Invest in Women Internationally

Elaine Zuckerman, President, Gender Action

Working as a project economist on China for the World Bank during the 1980s, I designed and monitored rural microcredit projects for the bank's largest client. I was struck by the fact that 100 percent of loan documents were signed by men in the poor peasant households that I visited. When I travel today into the hinterlands of China and other Asian and African countries, I see that men still sign off on and use most loans. Men also run the banks.

Over 70 percent of the world's poor are women, most of whom live in rural areas. In Africa, where 80 percent of farmers are women, women receive less than 10 percent of the credit reaching small farmers and only 1 percent of the total credit reaching the agricultural sector.[11] When women do get credit, their average loan size is smaller than that of their male counterparts.

Entrenched and sexist lending practices generally deny women access to credit, despite much evidence demonstrating that poor women use and repay microcredit loans better than men do.[12] Many women who access credit lift their households out of poverty by effectively managing small loans.

This microcredit picture represents a much broader and deeper problem. In numerous countries, women lack rights to conduct business, own property, or even travel without their husbands' consent. A number of countries have passed laws granting women these rights, but the laws are hardly implemented because of persistent discrimination against women who lack information about their rights.

The World Bank's own research demonstrates compelling correlations among greater gender equality, greater economic growth, and less poverty in countries worldwide. All six international financial institutions (IFIs), including the World Bank, have made it a primary mission to enhance growth and reduce poverty. Nevertheless, the IFIs' "big bucks" invest-ments, amounting to almost a trillion dollars over the last 60 years,[13] per-petuate deep gender inequalities. A year 2000 World Bank review of 3,028 World Bank loan agreements concluded that only 7 percent referred to, let alone analyzed, gender or women's roles.[14] The World Bank made roughly $18 billion in annual disbursements, out of which it allo-cated a mere $600,000 to facilitate implementing its new 2001 "Gender Strategy."[15]

Billions of dollars of IFI infrastructure loans have financed trans-portation and water supply systems. These loans have hardly addressed the problem that women in the poorest countries still spend hours every day carrying water (usually on their heads) while walking barefoot on unpaved roads. In fact, women undertake almost all domestic transporta-tion tasks in the poorest countries. In Zambia, 96 percent of domestic travel time is attributed to women, only 1 percent to men, and 3 percent to children.[16] This pattern is repeated across poor countries. Nevertheless, women lack access to basic vehicles, even to bicycles, wheelbarrows, and pull carts, whereas men, whose domestic transportation needs are much smaller, have greater access to such vehicles. But this is just one example of an opportunity to support and invest in women and their potential around the globe.

⇉ CALL TO ACTION ⇇

+ Call or write your representative in Congress and your senators to ask them to attach conditions to their grants to the IFIs requiring these institutions to promote and monitor women's rights and gen-der equality in their transportation, water, microcredit, and all other loans to poor countries.

+ Learn more about the gendered impacts of IFI investments at www.genderaction.org. Support our campaign to ensure that IFI investments promote women's rights and gender equality by making a financial contribution or helping with fundraising.

- Learn more about and support microcredit for poor women through the Grameen Foundation USA (www.gfusa.org), the Microcredit Summit Campaign (www.microcreditsummit.org), and Women's World Banking (www.swwb.org). These organizations work to ensure that the world's low-income families, especially women, receive credit for self-employment and business services.

Afterword:

Women at the Global Decision-Making Table

Madeleine K. Albright

It wasn't that long ago, even in the United States, when women were not permitted to vote. We had virtually no voice in government, the professions or academia. And our clothes were designed by structural engineers. Until 30 years ago, women in the U.S. Foreign Service had to resign if they committed the crime of getting married.

Around the globe, it was extremely rare to see a woman in a top job. We did not have many role models. There was Queen Elizabeth, but it is hard to work your way up to the position of queen. There were Indira Gandhi and Benazir Bhutto, who first became known because of their famous families, but for most of us, it was too late to choose famous parents. My personal favorites were Golda Meir, a schoolteacher in Milwaukee who became prime minister of Israel, and Margaret Thatcher, whose politics I did not share but whose style answered forever the question of whether a woman could be tough.

Today, I have the honor of chairing a group of women who have served in cabinet positions around the world. We have hundreds of members and are growing rapidly as more and more women are chosen for top positions. It is equally important that qualified women fill sub-cabinet jobs — as parliamentarians and mayors, judges and party officials. To this end, we should support organizations around the world that are striving to equip women in emerging democracies with the skills they need to participate and succeed.

These organizations are able to train women candidates in campaign planning and public speaking, media relations and fundraising. They help women legislators develop computer expertise, learn how to draft bills, and master parliamentary procedure. They give women the confidence to put themselves forward. Each step counts, because there is a direct connection between the success of women in government and the success of women outside government.

If women in government do their jobs, they will help improve the fate of women and girls everywhere. They will raise issues that others overlook, pass bills that others oppose, put money into projects that others ignore and seek to end abuses that others tolerate.

When I was U.S. ambassador to the United Nations, I formed a club with the other women ambassadors – a very small club. We called ourselves the G-7. But we magnified our influence by agreeing to always take each other's phone calls. When I was secretary of state, I made the same arrangements among women foreign ministers. When some of the men complained that diplomats from Barbados or Liechtenstein, for example, had speedier access to my office than they did, I said there was a simple solution to their problem. They could have themselves replaced by women. They never complained again.

These clubs, though small, did make a difference. For example, we helped ensure the appointment of women justices and prosecutors to the Balkans' war crimes tribunal. This mattered because so many of the crimes being investigated had been committed against women. The result was that rape, for the first time, was classified as a war crime.

In 1999, the women foreign ministers issued a worldwide call for action to curb trafficking in human beings. The following year, we proposed a series of actions designed to halt the spread of HIV/AIDS. Women can also act together on the global stage to increase support for international family planning services and reproductive health care. Each of these initiatives can lift the lives of women and girls and thereby help communities and whole countries to flourish.

For inspiration, we should remind ourselves every day that each time a law is changed to ensure women's rights, or a policy is changed to ensure that girls are educated, or a budget is changed to give women in need a helping hand, or a mind is changed to help elect a woman to high political office, we make the process of change work for us and shrink the distance to the goals toward which we are climbing.

Years ago, Margaret Mead urged us never to "doubt that a small group of thoughtful, committed citizens can change the world. Indeed, it's the only thing that ever has." Our group today is no longer so small. But we are thoughtful, and we are committed. Have no doubt, we are changing the world.

Endnotes

Section 1

1   American Lung Association. *State of the Air Report.* 2004.

2   Environmental Protection Agency. February 2004.

3   National Academy of Sciences. "Toxicological Effects of Methylmercury." 2000.

4   National Council of Women's Organizations. "American Women in the 21st Century, the Facts: On Women and Health Insurance." 2004. Available at: www.womensorganizations.org/pages.cfm?ID—78.

5   M. Lethbridge-Çejku, J.S. Schiller, and L. Bernadel. National Health Interview Survey, Division of Health Interview Statistics. Summary Health Statistics for U.S. Adults, Appendix III, Table XVI. 2002.

6   Jeanne M. Lambrew. *Diagnosing Disparities in Health Insurance for Women: A Prescription for Change* 4 (based on 1997 CPS data). New York: The Commonwealth Fund. 2001.

7   Over 30 percent of Latina women and over 20 percent of African American women are uninsured, compared to 13 percent of white women. Data are for health insurance coverage of women ages 18 to 64 in 1999. Women's Health Insurance Coverage, *supra* note 7.

8   Including but not limited to: the American Medical Student Association (www.amsa.org) and Physicians for a National Health Program (www.pnhp.org).

9   Available at: www.grahamazon.com/sp/other.php.

10   Alan Guttmacher Institute. "State Facts About Abortion." 2003. Available at: www.agi-usa.org/pubs/sfaa.html.

11   National Abortion Federation. "Incidents of Violence and Disruption against Abortion Providers." 2004. Available at: www.prochoice.org.

12   Joan Biskupic. "Abortion Could Be a 'Phony War.'" *USA Today.* June 4, 2002.

13   Gloria Feldt. *Behind Every Choice Is a Story.* Denton, TX: University of North Texas Press. 2002. p. 53.

14   Gloria Feldt. *The War on Choice: The Right-Wing Attack on Women's*

Lives and How to Fight Back. New York: Bantam. 2004. p. 10. See also www.waronchoice.com.

15 Advocates for Youth, Sexuality Information and Education Council of the United States (SIECUS)."Toward a Sexually Healthy America: Roadblocks Imposed by the Federal Government's Abstinence-Only-Until-Marriage Education Program." Available at: www.advocatesforyouth. org/publications/abstinenceonly.pdf.

16 CBS News Poll. May 20-23, 2004. Asked,"Which of these comes closest to your view? Abortion should be generally available to those who want it. Abortion should be available, but under stricter limits than it is now. OR, Abortion should not be permitted," 36 percent of respondents said abortion should be generally available; 37 percent said it should remain legal, though under stricter limits. Only 25 percent said it should be outlawed.

17 American Psychological Association: www.apa.org/monitor/oct01/ eating.html.

18 For modest weight loss statistics on a popular weight loss pill, see: D.E. Arterburn, P.K. Crane, and D.L. Veenstra."The Efficacy and Safety of Sibutramine for Weight Loss: A Systemic Review. *Archives in Internal Medicine.* Vol. 164: pp. 994-1003. 2004. For information about risks, see www.citizen.org/pressroom/release.cfm?ID=1533.

19 S.Wolfe."Ephedra Scientific Evidence versus Money/Politics." *Science.* April 18, 2003. Available at: www.citizen.org/publications/release. cfm?ID=7241 and www.citizen.org/pressroom/release.cfm?ID=1617.

20 Available at: www.ftc.gov/opa/2003/07/wellquest.htm.

21 Available at: www.surgery.org/press/statistics.php.

22 E.L.Weiss, J.G.Longhurst, and C.M.Mazure."Childhood Sexual Abuse as a Risk Factor for Depression in Women: Psychosocial and Neurobiological Correlates." *American Journal of Psychiatry.* 156: pp. 816-828. 1999.

23 D.Belle."Social Ties and Social Support." In D.Belle (ed.), *Lives in Stress: Women and Depression.* Beverly Hills, CA: Sage. 1982. See also: C.M. Mazure, G.P.Keita, and M.C.Blehar."Summit on Women and Depression: Proceedings and Recommendations."Washington, D.C.: American Psychological Association. 2002.

24 S.J.Borowsky, L.V.Rubenstein, L.S.Meredith, P.Camp, M.Jackson-Triche, and K.B.Wells."Who Is at Risk of Nondetection of Mental Health Prob-

lems in Primary Care?" *Journal of General Internal Medicine.* 15: pp. 381–388. 2000.

25 D.G. Blazer, R.C. Kessler, K.A. McGonagle, and M.S. Swartz. The Prevalence and Distribution of Major Depression in a National Community Sample: The National Cororbidity Survey. *American Journal of Psychiatry.* 151: pp. 979-986. 1994.

26 U.S. Census Bureau. Annual Demographic Survey, March (2003) Supplement to Current Population Survey, Table HI01. Available at: http://ferret.bls.census.gov/macro/032003/health/h01-001.htm.

27 Ibid.

28 U.S. Census Bureau. "Historical Income Tables–People." Table P-8. Available at: www.census.gov/hhes/income/histinc/p08.html.

29 Bureau of Labor Statistics. "Age of Reference Person: Average Annual Expenditures and Characteristics." Table 3, Consumer Expenditure Survey, 2001–2002. Available at: www.bls.gov/cex/2003/Standard/age.pdf.

30 "Older Adults and Mental Health." *Mental Health: A Report to the Surgeon General.* Available at: www.surgeongeneral.gov/library/mental health/chapter5/sec1.html.

31 M.C. Blehar and D.A. Oren. "Gender Differences in Depression." *Medscape Women's Health* 2: p. 3. 1997. Revised from "Women's Increased Vulnerability to Mood Disorders: Integrating Psychobiology and Epidemiology." *Depression.* 3: pp. 3-12. 1995.

Section 2

1 U.S. Department of Labor, Bureau of Labor Statistics. "Employment Characteristics of Families in 2002." Tables 5 and 6, Current Population Survey. 2003. Available at: www.bls.gov/news.release/pdf/famee.pdf. These percentages understate how many women raising children are in the paid labor force because they reflect only women raising their *own* children and do not include the many women who are raising grandchildren, nieces and nephews, or other related children. Note that the labor force includes those who are working and those who are looking for work.

2 K. Smith. "Who's Minding the Kids? Child Care Arrangements: Spring 1997." Current Population Reports 70-86. July 2002.

3 Ewan and Hart, *supra* note 2, at 74.

4 K. Schulman. *The High Cost of Child Care Puts Quality Care out of Reach for Many Families.* Washington, D.C.: Children's Defense Fund. 2000.

5   National Women's Law Center. *States Limit Child Care Help for Low-Income Working Families.* Washington, D.C.: National Women's Law Center. 2004. The report cites information from state child care administrators and policy leaders collected by the National Women's Law Center in early 2004; unpublished information collected by the Children's Defense Fund in the fall of 2003; and two published reports by the Children's Defense Fund, *State Budget Cuts Create a Growing Child Care Crisis for Low-Income Working Families* (March 2003) and *State Developments in Child Care, Early Education, and School-Age Care* 2002 (April 2003).

6   National Women's Law Center. *Making Care Less Taxing: Improving State Child and Dependent Care Tax Provisions.* Washington, D.C.: National Women's Law Center. 2002. See also: National Women's Law Center. *2004 Supplement to Making Care Less Taxing.* Washington, D.C.: National Women's Law Center. 2004.

7   Karen Schulman. *Key Facts: Essential Information about Child Care, Early Education and School-Age Care.* Washington, D.C.: Children's Defense Fund. 2003. p. 3. The report cites the National Household Education Survey from the U.S. Department of Education, National Center for Education Statistics.

8   Danielle Ewen and Katherine Hart. *State Developments in Child Care, Early Education, and School-Age Care* 2002. Washington, D.C.: Children's Defense Fund. 2002. Available at: www.childrensdefense.org.

9   Data were gathered by Fight Crime: Invest in Kids, a group of more than 2,000 police chiefs, sheriffs, leaders of police associations, prosecutors, victims of violence, and members of youth violence organizations. See www.fightcrime.org.

10 Corporate Voices for Working Families. *Afterschool for All: A Call to Action from the Business Community.* 2004. Available at: www.cvworkingfamilies.org.

11 Ibid.

12 For the results of a five-year evaluation of programs run by the After-School Corporation, see www.tascorp.org/mediacenter/press-releases/evaluation. See also: Beth Miller. *Critical Hours: Afterschool Programs and Educational Success.* Boston: Nellie Mae Education Foundation. 2003.

13 See, for example: MGT of America, Inc. "The Economic Impact of Child Care in Florida." Florida's Children's Forum. 2003. Available at: www.flchild.com. See also: Louise Stoney, Mildred Warner, et al. "Investing in the Child Care Industry: An Economic Development Strategy for

Kansas." Mid-America Regional Council. 2003. Available at: www.marc. org/mccc/kseconimpactreportfinal.pdf. See also: Saskia Traill and Jen Wohl. "The Economic Impact of the Child Care and Early Education Industry in Massachusetts." National Economic Development and Law Center. 2004. Available at: www.doe.mass.edu/els/news04/nedlc-report. pdf.

14 Vicky Lovell. *No Time to Be Sick: Why Everyone Suffers When Workers Don't Have Paid Sick Leave.* Institute for Women's Policy Research. May 2004. p.1.

15 Kaiser Family Foundation. "Women, Work and Family Health: A Balancing Act." Issue Brief. April 2003. Available at: www.kff.org.

16 Jody Heymann. *The Widening Gap: Why America's Working Families Are in Jeopardy and What Can Be Done about It.* Basic Books. 2000.

17 R.C. Barnett and K. Gareis. *Parental After-School Stress Project.* Community, Families & Work Program, Brandeis University. 2004. Summary available at: www.bcfwp.org.

18 For example, in 1999–2000, teenaged mothers were only 8.1 percent of all adults on the welfare rolls. Source: U.S. Department of Health and Human Services. *Temporary Assistance for Needy Families (TANF) Program: Fourth Annual Report to Congress.* Washington, D.C. 2001.

19 An IWPR report found that, even before the 1996 welfare reform, almost half of mothers who received welfare also worked. Source: Roberta Spalter-Roth, Beverly Burr, Heidi Hartmann, and Lois Shaw. *Welfare That Works: The Working Lives of AFDC Recipients.* Washington, D.C. 1995.

20 Deanna M. Lyter, Melissa Sills, Gi-Taik Oh, and Avis Jones-DeWeever. *The Children Left Behind: Deeper Poverty, Fewer Supports.* Washington, D.C.: Institute for Women's Policy Research. 2004.

21 *Report of the UN Commission on the Status of Women.* February 28, 2000.

22 Ibid.

23 P. Tjaden and N. Thoennes. *Full Report of the Prevalence, Incidence, and Consequences of Intimate Partner Violence against Women: Findings from the National Violence against Women Survey.* Washington, D.C.: National Institute of Justice. 2000. Available at: www.ncjrs.org.

24 Ibid.

25 Florida Governor's Task Force on Domestic and Sexual Violence. *Florida Mortality Review Project.* Table 15. p.46. 1997.

26 For example, Tracy Huling found that 59% of women in New York committed to prison in 1986 for killing someone close to them were being

abused at the time of the crime: T. Huling, *Breaking the Silence*, New York: Correctional Association of New York, 1991, cited in J. Pollock, *Counseling Women in Prison*, CA: Sage Publications, 1998, 15.

27 Available at: www.berghof-handbook.net.

28 Save the Children. *State of the World's Mothers* 2002. pp. 7–8. Available at: www.savethechildren.org/publications/sowm2002.pdf.

Section 3

1 National Center for Education Statistics. 1999–2000.

2 W. Judy and Carol D'Amico. *Workforce 2020: Work and Workers in the 21st Century*. Washington, D.C.: Hudson Institute. 1997.

3 National Women's Studies Association data bank. Available at: www. nwsa.org.

4 U.S. Census Bureau. Available at: www.census.gov/prod/2004pubs/censr-15.pdf.

5 Wider Opportunities for Women (WOW). "Coming Up Short: A Comparison of Wages and Work Supports in 10 American Communities." July 22, 2004.

6 Ford Foundation. *Work-Family Issues and Low-Income Families*. Summer 2000.

7 American Cancer Society. *Cancer Facts and Figures*. 2004.

8 E. White. "Glut of Cause Marketing Draws Critics in Industry." *Wall Street Journal*. October 16, 2002.

9 Available at: www.yoplait.com/breastcancer_lids.aspx.

10 Available at: www.thinkbeforeyoupink.org/Pages/CosmeticCompanies.html.

11 U.S. Food and Drug Administration. Office of Cosmetics Fact Sheet. February 3, 1995. Available at: http://vm.cfsan.fda.gov/~dms/cos-206.html.

12 P.D. Darbe. "Concentrations of Parabens in Human Breast Tumors." *Journal of Applied Toxicology*. 24, 1: pp. 5–13. 2004.

13 Available at: www.ewg.org/briefings/acc.

14 U.S. Census Bureau. Analysis of 2000 data.

15 Center for Women's Business Research. *Key Facts about Women-Owned Businesses*. 2004.

16 National Foundation for Women Business Owners. 2000.

17 Ibid.

Section 4

1 Jenny Toomey. "Empire of the Air," *The Nation*. January 2003.

2 Poytner Institute. "The American Journalist Study." April 2003.

3 Women's Voices, Women's Vote Project. See www.wvwv.org.

4 See www.utne.com, www.encyclopedia.thefreedictionary.com, *Women's E-News* (www.womensenews.org/article.cfm/dyn/aid/1805/context/cover), and *National NOW Times* (www.now.org).

5 Gary F. Moncrief, Peverill Squire, and Malcolm E. Jewell. *Who Runs for the Legislature?* New York: Pearson Education. 2000.

6 Ruth B. Mandel and Katherine E. Kleeman. *Political Generation Next: America's Young Elected Leaders.* Eagleton Institute of Politics, Rutgers University. 2004.

7 Linda J. Sax et al. *The American Freshman: National Norms for Fall 2003.* University of California, Los Angeles, Graduate School of Education & Information Studies. December 2003.

8 U.S. Department of Defense, Defense Manpower Data Center. Unpublished data. September 30, 2003.

9 "Military Women as UN Peacekeepers." Available at: http://userpages.aug.com/captbarb/degroot.html.

10 "Views of the American People on Equal Rights for Male and Female Citizens." Survey conducted for the ERA Campaign Network (www.ERA Campaign.net) by Opinion Research Corporation (ORC) Caravan Services. July 2001.

11 Ibid.

12 Marie C. Wilson. *Closing the Leadership Gap.* Viking Books. 2004.

13 The White House Project. Available at: www.thewhitehouseproject.org/know_facts/snapshots_women.html.

14 Christopher Hellman. "Last of the Big Time Spenders: U.S. Military Budget Is the World's Largest, and Still Growing." Center for Arms Control and Non-Proliferation.

Section 5

1 C. Mast. *Sex Respect: The Option of True Sexual Freedom.* Bradley, IL: Respect, Inc. 2001. Student workbook, p. 131.

2 M. Gallagher Duran. *Reasonable Reasons to Wait: The Keys to Character.* Chantilly, VA: A Choice in Education. 2002-2003. Student workbook, p. 96.

3 *Art of Loving Well: A Character Education Curriculum for Today's Teenager.* Boston: The Loving Well Project, Boston University School of Education. 1993. Teacher's guide, p. 31.

4 C. Mast. *Sex Respect: The Option of True Sexual Freedom.* Bradley, IL: Respect, Inc. 2001. Student workbook, p. 80.

5 Ibid.

6 M. Gallagher Duran. *Reasonable Reasons to Wait: The Keys to Character.* Chantilly, VA: A Choice in Education. 2002-2003. Student workbook, p. 96.

7 J. Grunbaum et. al. "Surveillance Summaries: Youth Risk Behavior Surveillance — United States, 2003." *Morbidity and Mortality Weekly Report.* Vol. 53, No. SS-2: pp. 1-95. May 21, 2004. Available at: www.cdc.gov/nccdphp/dash/yrbs.

8 D. Kirby. *Emerging Answers: Research Findings on Programs to Reduce Teen Pregnancy.* Washington, D.C.: The National Campaign to Prevent Teen Pregnancy. May 2001.

9 American Psychological Association. *Violence and the Family: Report of the APA Presidential Task Force on Violence and the Family.* p. 40. 1996.

10 Joan Zorza. *Protecting the Children in Custody Disputes When One Parent Abuses the Other.* 29 Clearinghouse Rev. 1113. 1996.

11 Ibid.

12 Cathy Schoen et al. *The Commonwealth Fund Survey for the Health of Adolescent Girls.* November 1997.

13 C. Krulewitch. "Prevalence of Domestic Violence among Women Seeking Abortion Services." *Women's Health Issues.* Vol. 4: pp. 204-9. 1996.

14 NBC News/ *Wall Street Journal* poll. January 2003. Also: *USA Today*/CNN/Gallup poll as reported in *USA Today.* January 7, 2003.

15 Center for Gender Equality. *Progress and Perils: How Gender Issues Unite and Divide Women.* October 2001. Available at: www.advancewomen.org/womens_research/PartOne.pdf.

16 D. Sabo, K.E. Miller, M.J. Melnick, and L. Heywood. *Her Life Depends on It: Sport, Physical Activity, and the Health and Well-Being of American Girls.* East Meadow, NY: Women's Sports Foundation. 2004.

17 National Center for Health Statistics. *Health, United States, 2002.* Hyattsville, MD. 2002.

18 S.K. Henshaw. *U.S. Teenage Pregnancy Statistics with Comparative Statistics for Women Aged 20–24.* New York: The Alan Guttmacher Institute.

2003. See also: National Campaign to Prevent Teen Pregnancy. *Not Just Another Single Issue: Teen Pregnancy Prevention's Link to Other Critical Social Issues.* Washington, D.C. 2002.

19   The Commonwealth Fund. "Survey Finds Missed Opportunities to Improve Girls' Health." *Commonwealth Fund Quarterly* 3 (3). 1997. Available at: www.cmwf.org/publist/quarterly/fas97qrt.asp?link=6.

20   G.B. Schreiber et al. "Weight Modification Efforts Reported by Black and White Preadolescent Girls: National Heart, Lung, and Blood Institute Growth and Health Study." *Pediatrics.* 98 (1): pp. 63-70. 1996.

21   Centers for Disease Control and Prevention. "Annual Smoking-Attributable Mortality, Years of Potential Life Lost, and Economic Costs – United States, 1995-1999." *Morbidity and Mortality Weekly Report.* 51: pp. 300-303. 2002.

22   U.S. Department of Health and Human Services, Office of the Surgeon General. Women and Smoking: A Report of the Surgeon General. 2001.

23   Available at: www.4woman.gov/minority/leading.htm.

24   L.K. Bunker. "Life-Long Benefits of Youth Sport Participation for Girls and Women." Presented at the Sport Psychology Conference, University of Virginia, Charlottesville. June 22, 1988.

25   *Game Face, from the Locker Room to the Boardroom: A Survey on Sports in the Lives of Women Business Executives.* February 2002.

26   National Federation of State High School Associations. *NFHS Handbook* 2003-2004. Indianapolis, IN: National Federation of State High School Associations. 2003. See also: National Collegiate Athletic Association. Participation Statistics. 2001-2002. Available at: www.ncaa.org.

27   L.K. Bunker. "Life-Long Benefits of Youth Sport Participation for Girls and Women." Presented at the Sport Psychology Conference, University of Virginia, Charlottesville. June 22, 1988.

28   Centers for Disease Control and Prevention. "Surveillance Summaries." *Morbidity and Mortality Weekly Report.* Vol. 51, No. SS-4. 2002.

29   Zittleman and Sadker. American University. 2002.

30   W.B. Fritz. "The Women of ENIAC." *IEEE Annals of the History of Computing.* Vol. 18, No. 3: pp. 13-28. 1996.

31   P.B. Campbell and J.N. Storo. *Girls Are ... Boys Are ...: Myths, Stereotypes & Gender Differences.* U.S. Department of Education, Office of Educational Research and Improvement.

Section 6

1 Martha Langelan. *Back Off: How to Confront and Stop Sexual Harassment and Harassers.* New York: Simon and Schuster. 1993. p. 45.
2 Ibid., pp. 97–104.
3 Gallup Organization. May 10-14, 2001.
4 Lambda Legal Defense Fund. Available at: www.lambdalegal.org.
5 Available at: www.civilrightsproject.harvard.edu/research/reseg03/resegregation03.php.
6 National Center for Health Statistics and Centers for Disease Control and Prevention. *National Vital Statistics Report.* Data compiled by the Brady Center to Prevent Gun Violence. November 4, 2003.
7 Centers for Disease Control and Prevention. *Morbidity and Mortality Weekly Report.* February 7, 1997.
8 A.L. Kellerman et al. *New England Journal of Medicine.* 1993. See also: A.L. Kellerman. *Journal of Trauma.* 1998.
9 Brady Center to Prevent Gun Violence. *On Target: The Impact of the 1994 Federal Assault Weapons Act.* Available at: www.bradycenter.org.
10 U.S. Department of Labor, Bureau of Labor Statistics. *BLS News:* 04-148.
11 K. Bronfenbrenner. "Organizing Women Workers in the Global Economy: Findings from NLRB Certification Elections – 1998-1999." 2001.
12 U.S. Department of Labor, Bureau of Labor Statistics. *BLS News:* 04-148.
13 U.S. Department of Labor, Bureau of Labor Statistics. *BLS News:* 04-02.
14 AFL-CIO. "The Silent War: The Assault on Workers' Freedom to Choose a Union and Bargain Collectively in the U.S." Issue Brief. 2002.
15 U.S. Department of Labor, Bureau of Labor Statistics. *BLS News:* 04-02.

Section 7

1 *Report of the UN Commission on the Status of Women.* February 28, 2000.
2 UNESCO Institute for Statistics. September 2004.
3 Amy O'Neill Richard. *A Contemporary Manifestation of Slavery and Organized Crime.* An intelligence monograph international trafficking in women to the U.S. April 2000.
4 *Report on Maternal Mortality* developed by WHO, UNICEF, and UNFPA. 2000.
5 Joint United Nations Programme on HIV/AIDS. 2002.
6 Senate Foreign Relations Committee hearing. June 13, 2002. S. Hrg. 107-530, transcript p. 33.

7   U.S. Department of State. *Trafficking in Persons Report* 2004. Available at: www.state.gov/g/tip/rls/tiprpt/2004.

8   Choike.org. "Bush Administration Launches New Battle in the War on Women." Available at: www.choike.org/nuevo_eng/informes/1757.html.

9   Choike.org. "Sexual and Reproductive Rights." Available at: www.choike. org/nuevo_eng/informes/1197.html.

10   International Working Group on Sexuality and Social Policy. "Global Implications of U.S. Domestic and International Policies on Sexuality." Available at: www.unwire.org/UNWire/20040628/449_25318.asp.

11   C. Mark Blackden and Chitra Bhanu. "Gender, Growth, and Poverty Reduction: Special Program of Assistance for Africa." *1998 Status Report on Poverty in Sub-Saharan Africa.* Washington, D.C.: World Bank Africa Region. 1999.

12   Of the many publications verifying that women are a better credit risk and use loans better than men do, one of the author's favorites is: David Bornstein. *The Price of a Dream: The Story of the Grameen Bank and the Idea That Is Helping the Poor to Change Their Lives.* New York: Simon and Schuster. 1999.

13   Data from the Bank Information Center, a nonprofit advocacy group in Washington, D.C.

14   Operations Evaluation Department. "Integrating Gender in World Bank Assistance." World Bank. 2000.

15   Elaine Zuckerman and Wu Qing. *Reforming the World Bank: Will the New Gender Strategy Make a Difference?* Heinrich Böll Foundation North America. 2003. Available at: www.genderaction.org.

16   Mark Blackden. "Integrating Gender into Poverty Reduction Strategy Papers (PRSPs) in Sub-Saharan Africa: A Win-Win Scenario." Slide Presentation. World Bank Office of the Africa Region Chief Economist. March 2001.

Resources

PRESERVE A HEALTHY ENVIRONMENT

The organization Clear the Air (www.cleartheair.org) was jointly created by environmental advocacy groups to bring public attention to the problem of air pollution. You can also get information on other environmental issues from the National Environmental Trust (www.net.org), the Sierra Club (www.sierraclub.org), the Natural Resources Defense Council (www.nrdc.org), and the U.S. Public Interest Research Group (www.uspirg.org). These organizations are ready and willing to help individuals and communities organize on issues.

ENSURE SEXUAL HEALTH

Lend your time and money to the following women's organizations, which support choice, sex education, and women's health issues: Black Women's Health Imperative (www.blackwomenshealth.org), Catholics for a Free Choice (www.cath4choice.org), Center for Reproductive Rights (www.crlp.org), Cover My Pills (www.covermypills.org), Feminist Majority Foundation (www.feminist.org), International Planned Parenthood Federation (www.ippf.org), International Women's Health Coalition (www.iwhc.org), NARAL Pro-Choice America (www.naral.org), National Abortion Federation (www.prochoice.org), National Asian Pacific American Women's Forum (www.napawf.org), National Asian Women's Health Organization (www.nawho.org), National Council of Jewish Women (www.ncjw.org), National Council for Negro Women (www.ncnw.org), National Latina Institute for Reproductive Health (www.latinainstitute.org), National Organization for Women (www.now.org), National Partnership for Women and Families (www.nationalpartnership.org), National Women's Law Center (www.nwlc.org), Planned Parenthood Federation of America (www.plannedparenthood.org), Religious Coalition for Reproductive Choice (www.rcrc.org), saveROE (www.saveroe.com), and Vox: Voices for Planned Parenthood (www. plannedparenthood.org/vox).

PROVIDE ACCESS TO MENTAL HEALTH CARE

If you know someone who needs mental health care, the National Mental Health Association provides referrals for local treatment services at no cost. To find a mental health specialist in your area, call 1-800-969-6642.

The Health and Human Services Department has put together a comprehensive tool kit of mental health resources for the aging called "Get Connected." To order it at no cost, email info@health.org or call 1-800-729-6686.

END THE ERA OF LATCHKEY CHILDREN

To learn more about organizations working to improve after-school care, go to the following websites: www.familyinitiative.org, www.after schoolalliance.org, www.fightcrime.org, and www.cvworkingfamil ies.org.

For more on this issue, read Joan Lombardi's *Time to Care: Redesigning Child Care to Promote Education, Support Families, and Build Communities* (Temple University Press, 2003).

STOP DOMESTIC VIOLENCE

The website www.4woman.gov/violence and Karen J. Wilson's book *When Violence Begins at Home* both offer information on spotting signs of abuse.

If you or anyone you know has suffered abuse or been threatened with it, call one of these hotlines: the National Resource Center on Domestic Violence Hotline (1-800-537-2238), the National Domestic Violence Hotline (1-800-799-7233; Spanish: 1-800-942-6908; TTD: 1-800-787-3224), the National Sexual Assault Hotline (1-800-656-4673), the National Child Abuse Hotline (1-800-422-4453), and the National Elder Abuse Hotline (1-866-363-4276).

WomensLaw.org (www.womenslaw.org) is an online resource that provides state-specific legal information and resources for women living with or escaping domestic violence.

The National Women's Health Information Center (www.4women. org) offers a state-by-state listing of places where women can get help. Call 1-800-994-9662 or 1-888-220-5446.

Since its inception in 1995, the Violence Against Women Office has handled the legal and policy issues regarding violence against women for the Department of Justice, and responded to requests for information regarding violence against women. For more information, call (1-202-307-6026), fax (1-202-307-3911), or visit the website (www.ojp.usdoj.gov/vawo/welcome.html).

The National Youth Violence Prevention Resource Center, a central source of information on prevention and intervention programs, makes available publications, research, and statistics on violence committed by and against children and teens. Contact the center online (www.safe youth.org) or by phone (1-866-723-3968).

The National Center for Elder Abuse provides information about elder abuse and offers technical assistance and training to elder abuse agencies and related professionals. Contact the center by phone (1-202-898-2586) or email (ncea@nasua.org), or visit online (www.elderabuse center.org).

Other organizations that can help include the National Coalition Against Domestic Violence (www.ncadv.org) and the Family Violence Prevention Fund (1-415-252-8900; online: www.endabuse.org).

PROMOTE FINANCIAL LITERACY

For a wealth of information on financial literacy visit www.fdic.gov, www.dol.gov/wb, or www.ncadv.com. For home-buying and credit guides in nine languages visit www.fanniemaefoundation.org and click on publications.

ADVOCATE FOR WOMEN IN THE MEDIA

Join the online alert lists of organizations and publications working to reform the media, including Common Cause (www.commoncause.org), Fairness & Accuracy in Reporting (www.fair.org), the Feminist Majority (www.feminist.org), Free Press (www.freepress.net), *Herizons* magazine (www.herizons.ca), *Ms.* magazine (www.msmagazine.com), the

National Organization for Women (www.now.org), and the magazine
Women & Environments International (www.weimag.com).

RECOGNIZE WOMEN IN THE MILITARY

For more information on women in the military or women veterans, see
the website www.wrei.org and the following publications of the Women's
Research & Education Institute: *Women in the Military: Where They
Stand* and *Women Veterans Employment*.

REASSESS NATIONAL PRIORITIES

For background information to assist you in taking action, read the booklet "A Safer, Better World Begins with Women ... It Begins with You" by
WAND and Women's Edge Coalition. This booklet explores more on
the federal budget and foreign policy issues related to women. You can
download it from www.wand.org or email info@wand.org. Fact sheets
on the federal budget, as well as information on women in elected office,
are also available on the WAND website.

   For data on what your community spends for housing, education,
health care, nuclear weapons, or the war in Iraq, check out www.national
priorities.org.

MENTOR WOMEN AND GIRLS

New Faces, More Voices is a leadership-training institute of the National
Council of Women's Organizations (NCWO). Launched during summer 1999, this program is designed to strengthen the women's movement
by providing leadership training and skill building for interns of NCWO
member organizations. For more information, visit www.womensorgani
zations.org.

   Women's Information Network (WIN) is a membership organization
created by a group of young women who were eager to find jobs and housing and to meet people who shared their interests. WIN creates regular
opportunities to mentor and share resources with like-minded women.
Visit the website at www.winonline.org.

   If you are in school, you can also use the Career Services Center at your
college or university to find a fellow alum working in your field.

LIBERATE GIRLS FROM ABUSE

To learn about services for teens and youth, please see Break the Cycle's website at www.break-the-cycle.org.

To receive a "Teen Dating Violence" resource kit, contact the National Resource Center on Domestic Violence by phone (1-800-537-2238) or online (www.nrcdv.org).

To learn about domestic violence services in your area, contact the National Domestic Violence Hotline (1-800-799-7233).

GAIN DAILY ACCESS TO SCIENCE AND TECHNOLOGY

The following organizations can help bring technology into the classroom: Autodesk (www.autodesk.com/dyf/dyfmain2.html), Girl Power (www.girlpower.gov/girlarea/sciencetech), Girl Tech (www.girltech.com), and Technology Standards for Teachers (www.cnets.iste.org/teachers).

To learn more about women who are leaders in specific fields, visit these websites: Women in Science (www.plugged-in.org/women_science.html), Women in Computer Science (www.sdsc.edu/CRAW/women.html), and the Women in Technology International Hall of Fame (www.witi.com/center/witimuseum/halloffame).

Brush up on the history of women in science and technology at the online museum of the Institute of Electrical and Electronic Engineers (www.ieee-virtual-museum.org/exhibit). For more resources, visit www.digital-sistas.org/resources.

ENGAGE IN A NEW WAVE OF ACTIVISM

To inspire yourself or young feminists you know, turn to these books about the next generation of feminism: *The Fire This Time: Young Activists and the New Feminism*, edited by Vivien Labaton and Dawn Lundy Martin; *Manifesta* by Amy Richards and Jennifer Baumgardner; and *Colonize This! Young Women of Color on Today's Feminism*, edited by Daisy Hernández and Bushra Rehman.

The following organizations, representing a broad spectrum of the feminist movement, encourage involvement by young activists: Active Element (www.activelement.org); Choice USA (www.choiceusa.org); Coalicion de Derechos Humanos (www.derechoshumanosaz.net); Committee on Women, Population, and the Environment (www.cwpe.org); Desis Rising Up and Moving (DRUM; www.drumnation.org); Exhale (www.4exhale.org); Funders' Collaborative on Youth Organizing (www.fcyo.org); INCITE! Women of Color Against Violence (www. incite-national.org); LISTEN, Inc.(www.lisn.org); League of Independent Voters (www.indyvoter.org); The Living Project (www.thelivingpro ject.org); Los Angeles Indigenous People's Alliance (www.laipa.net); Movement Strategy Center (www.movementstrategy.org); National Asian Pacific American Women's Forum (www.napawf.org); National Latina Institute for Reproductive Health (www.latinainstitute.org); National Women's Alliance (www.nwaforchange.org); Pro Choice Pub- lic Education Project (www.protectchoice.org); Resource Generation (www.resourcegeneration.org); School of Unity and Liberation (SOUL; www.youthec.org/soul); Sistas on the Rise (www.sistasontherise.org); SisterSong (www.sistersong.net); We Got Issues! (www.wegotissues. org); Young Women's Empowerment Project (www.youarepriceless.org); and Youth Action (www.youthaction.net).

VALUE DIVERSITY AND PROMOTE CULTURAL UNDERSTANDING

To support diversity in the women's movement, make a connection with one of these organizations: Asian Communities for Reproductive Justice (www.reproductivejustice.org), Asian Immigrant Women Advocates (www.aiwa.org), the Black Women's Health Imperative (www.black womenshealth.org), Khmer Girls in Action, the Latina Institute for Repro- ductive Justice (www.latinainstitute.org), National Asian Pacific Ameri- can Women's Forum (www.napawf.org), the National Women's Alliance (www.nwaforchange.org), Sistersong: Women of Color Reproductive Health Collective (www.sistersong.net), the Third Wave Foundation (www.thirdwavefoundation.org), and the Women of Color Resource Cen- ter (www.coloredgirls.org).

WAGE PEACE AROUND THE WORLD

Congress.org details all the committees for both the Senate and the House of Representatives and offers links to members' home pages with contact information. For international issues, the Senate committee is the Foreign

Relations Committee; for the House, it's the Committee on International Relations. And, of course, when it comes to setting funding priorities, the folks who determine the budget are always important: contact the Budget Committee in the Senate and the Committee on the Budget in the House.

IMPACT FOREIGN POLICY

To get involved in making a change on a global scale, link up with one of these organizations: Women's Environment and Development Organization (www.wedo.org) advocates for equality in global policy. CODEPINK (www.codepink4peace.org) fights for social justice and peace. Women organize for UNFPA at the website www.34millionfriends.org and for the state or municipal ratification of CEDAW at the site www.wildforhumanrights.org/cedaw_around_us.html.

ERADICATE RACISM

Black Women's Health Imperative (www.blackwomenshealth.org), Church Women United (www.churchwomen.org), Dialogue on Diversity (www.dialogueondiversity.org), MANA: A National Latina Organization (www.hermana.org), National Asian Pacific American Women's Forum (www.napawf.org), National Council of Negro Women (www.ncnw.org), and the National Latina Institute for Reproductive Health (www.latinainstitute.org).

Also support mainstream, predominantly white organizations working to eradicate racism, including the National Organization for Women (www.now.org) and the Young Women's Christian Association (www.ywca.org).

Contributors

Kiran Ahuja is the first national director of the National Asian Pacific American Women's Forum (NAPAWF), a progressive Asian Pacific American women's organization with a multi-issue advocacy focus. Visit www.napawf.org to find out about advocacy initiatives and NAPAWF chapters around the country.

Sarah C. Albert is the public policy director for the General Federation of Women's Clubs (www.gfwc.org). She also serves as cochair for the Working Group for the Ratification of CEDAW, a group of over 190 national nongovernmental organizations engaged in outreach and education to achieve U.S. ratification of the Treaty for the Rights of Women.

Madeleine K. Albright was named the 64th Secretary of State of the United States in 1997, becoming the first woman to hold that position and the highest ranking woman in the history of the U.S. government. As Secretary, Dr. Albright reinforced America's alliances, advocated democracy and human rights, and promoted American trade and business, labor, and environmental standards abroad. She is the founder of The Albright Group LLC, a global strategy firm and continues to lead at the international table.

Helen Blank is the director of leadership and public policy at the National Women's Law Center (www.nwlc.org). She has worked to strengthen child care policies for over 25 years, leading the effort at the federal level to enact the child care and development block grant. She has also authored numerous studies on early child development policies.

Mary Leigh Blek, PHN, serves as the president emeritus of the Million Mom March (www.millionmommarch.com). The Brady Campaign to Prevent Gun Violence united with the Million Mom March, a newly merged chapter-based grassroots organization, is dedicated to creating an America free from gun violence, where all Americans are safe at home, at school, at work, and in their communities.

Ellen Boneparth, Ph.D., is director of policy and programs at the National Council of Women's Organizations (www.ncwo-online.org). She was previously coordinator of women's studies and a professor of political science at San Jose State University and later dean of the College of Arts and Sciences at the University of Hawai'i, Hilo.

Martha Burk, Ph.D., is cofounder and president of the Center for Advancement of Public Policy in Washington, D.C., and currently serves as chair of the National Council of Women's Organizations (www.ncwo-online.org), a network of more than 200 groups collectively representing ten million women. Dr. Burk is also a syndicated columnist who appears often on radio and TV and a frequent contributor to electronic and print media, including *USA Today*, *The Nation*, *Ms.*, *Women's eNews*, and the *Washington Post*. Her book *Cult of Power: Sex Discrimination in Corporate America and What Can Be Done about It* will be published by Scribner in April 2005.

Leslie J. Calman is senior vice president of Legal Momentum (www.legal momentum.org), a women's legal rights organization. She directs Legal Momentum's Family Initiative, a campaign to educate, engage, and mobilize women and their families to advocate for quality child care, preschool, and after-school programs for every family who chooses them.

Lorraine Cole, Ph.D., is the president and chief executive officer of the Black Women's Health Imperative (www.blackwomenshealth.org), a leading national organization solely dedicated to ensuring optimum health for black women. Throughout her career, Dr. Cole has worked with health care providers, academic/research institutions, and health care consumers to eliminate racial disparities in health care.

Rosa L. DeLauro has represented the Third District of Connecticut in the House of Representatives since 1990. She serves on the Appropriations Committee and the Budget Committee, and in 1999, she was elected assistant to the Democratic Leader by her colleagues, making her the second-highest ranking Democratic woman in the House of Representatives. She currently serves as cochair of The Democratic Steering and Policy Committee, and has been a champion of policies to help women cope with the pressures of balancing work and family.

Dianne Feinstein, California's senior senator, was the first woman president of the San Francisco Board of Supervisors, the first woman mayor of San Francisco, the first woman elected senator of California, and the first woman member of the Senate Judiciary Committee. Feinstein has built a reputation as an independent voice, working with both Democrats and Republicans to find commonsense solutions to the problems facing our state and our nation.

Gloria Feldt is the president of the Planned Parenthood Federation of America (www.plannedparenthood.org) and of the Planned Parenthood Action Fund, the organization's political arm. She was once a young mother in West Texas in the days before the birth control pill and Roe v. Wade; her experience living without choice informs her advocacy and activism. She is the author of *The War on Choice: The Right-Wing Attack on Women's Rights and How to Fight Back.*

Kim Gandy is an attorney and president of the National Organization for Women (NOW) and the NOW Foundation. A longtime activist, Gandy has served NOW at local, state, and national levels since 1973, including three years as Louisiana NOW president. For more information, visit www.now.org and www.nowfoundation.org.

Lori Valencia Greene has been involved in politics since 1985, both as a Capitol Hill staffer and a lobbyist. Since 1996, she has been advocating on behalf of women and their families for the American Psychological Association.

Sarah Harder, president of the National Peace Foundation (www.national peace.org), works on peace-building projects in many regions of Russia. As a retired professor, past president of the American Association of University Women, and former vice president of the International Federation of University Women, she has worked with coalition leaders in 45 countries since 1980.

Cynthia Harrison is an associate professor of history, women's studies, and public policy at the George Washington University and a member of the Program Advisory Committee of the Institute for Women's Policy Research. She is the author of *On Account of Sex: The Politics of Women's Issues, 1945–1968.*

Heidi Hartmann is president of the Institute for Women's Policy Research (www.iwpr.org), an independent, nonprofit research organization that she founded in 1987. Dr. Hartmann earned a Ph.D. in economics from Yale in 1974, and in 1994 she received a MacArthur Fellowship. She is also research professor of women's studies and public policy at the George Washington University.

Mia Herndon is a program officer at the Third Wave Foundation. In the past, Mia has also worked in the areas of young women's leadership, international worker solidarity, countermilitary recruitment, and the criminalization/ imprisonment of people of color. She also acts and works as a labor assistant.

Dixie Horning is executive director of the UCSF National Center of Excellence in Women's Health (www.ucsf.edu/coe) and founding member of The Association of Academic Women's Health Programs (AAWHP). She was named the 2003 Distinguished Alumna by Texas A&M University. She is also the past chair of SeniorNet and the National Women's History Project.

Cindy Hounsell is the executive director of WISER, the Women's Institute for a Secure Retirement (www.wiser.heinz.org), a project launched by the Heinz Family Philanthropies in 1996. As executive director of the POWER-Center, the Program on Women's Education for Retirement, she trains leaders and grassroots advocates around the country.

Swanee Hunt lectures at Harvard's Kennedy School of Government. She is the former U.S. ambassador to Austria and the founder of Women Waging Peace, an initiative of The Hunt Alternatives Fund (www.womenwaging peace.net).

Nancy L. Hurlbert, president of Business and Professional Women/USA (www.bpwusa.org) is director of site engineering at Premier Commercial Realty, South Florida's third-largest commercial developer. Prior to joining Premier, she was a vice president with the prestigious engineering firm of Williams, Hatfield & Stoner, Inc. for nearly 30 years.

Patricia Ireland serves on the National Advisory Board of the Gender Public Advocacy Coalition (Gender PAC) and was president of the National Organization for Women from 1991 to 2001. Today she practices employment law in Washington, D.C.

Mal Johnson is a former White House and Capitol Hill correspondent with 35 years of experience in broadcast journalism. She serves on the boards of the Communications Consortium Media Center and the International Association of Women in Radio and Television. Inducted into the Journalists Hall of Fame in 1995, she is the cochair of the National Women's Conference and serves on the Steering Committee of the National Council of Women's Organizations.

Martha E. Kempner is the director of public information at SIECUS, the Sexuality Information and Education Council of the United States, where she helps shape the organization's message through its written materials and website (www.siecus.org). She received her master's degree in human sexuality from New York University.

Joan A. Kuriansky is executive director of Wider Opportunities for Women (www.wowonline.org). Long involved in promoting the rights of women, she cofounded the Campaign for Women's Health, served as executive director of the Older Women's League, and participated on President Clinton's National Advisory Council on Violence Against Women.

Marty Langelan is past president of the D.C. Rape Crisis Center and an internationally recognized expert on harassment, self-defense, and violence intervention. The author of *Back Off: How to Confront and Stop Sexual Harassment and Harassers*, she is also president of the National Woman's

Party, founded by suffragist Alice Paul to achieve full economic, legal, and political equity for women.

Donna A. Lopiano is the chief executive officer of the Women's Sports Foundation (www.WomensSportsFoundation.org), a national nonprofit organization founded by Billie Jean King, which works to advance the lives of girls and women through sports and physical activity.

Lisa M. Maatz is director of public policy and government relations for the American Association of University Women (www.aauw.org). As the organization's top policy advisor, she works to advance AAUW's issues on Capitol Hill. The recipient of two master's degrees, she also has an adjunct appointment to the Women and Politics Institute at American University.

Molly Murphy MacGregor is president and cofounder of the National Women's History Project (www.nwhp.org), which serves as the national clearinghouse for materials, resources, and other information related to multicultural women's history.

Carolyn B. Maloney represents the 14th district of New York in the U.S. Congress. She serves on the The Financial Services and Government Reform Committees. Maloney is former cochair of The Congressional Caucus for Women's Issues and has introduced the Equal Rights Amendment in Congress since 1997.

Captain Lory Manning, USN (retired) is director of the Women in the Military Project at the Women's Research and Education Institute (www.wrei.org). She serves on the Secretary of Veterans' Affairs Advisory Committee on Women Veterans.

Shireen Mitchell is the executive officer of Digital Sisters/Sistas (www.digital-sistas.org), a nonprofit organization providing technology education and enrichment for women and girls. Currently vice president of Community Technology Centers' Network, she has been recognized as an Outstanding Community Technology Leader and a Heroine in Technology.

Jill J. Morris is the director of the Public Policy Office of the National Coalition Against Domestic Violence (www.ncadv.org). She works closely with women's advocates at local, state, and national levels to identify the issues facing battered women, children, and service providers and to develop a legislative agenda to address these issues.

Karen O'Connor, Ph.D. and J.D., is the founder and director of the Women & Politics Institute at American University, where she is also a professor of government. She has authored or coauthored several books, including *Women, Politics and American Society* and *American Politics: Continuity and Change*.

Hedy M. Ratner is the copresident of the Women's Business Development Center (www.wbdc.org) in Chicago. She's been an activist and advocate for women's empowerment and economic power for the past 35 years.

Ileana Ros-Lehtinen was the first Hispanic woman elected to Congress. Born in Havana, Cuba, she fled to the United States with her family when she was seven years old. She serves on the International Relations and Government Reform Committees; her domestic policy priorities include education, senior citizens, women's health, victim's rights, and the environment.

Vicki Saporta is the president and chief executive officer of the National Abortion Federation (www.prochoice.org). Under Saporta's direction, NAF has played a critical role in protecting reproductive health care providers and in keeping abortion safe, legal, and accessible for women.

Jan Schakowsky, first elected to represent the 9th District of Illinois in 1998, serves on the House Energy and Commerce Committee and is chief deputy whip for the Democrats. She has fought for economic and social justice, for an end to violence against women, for a cleaner environment, and for national investment in health care, public education, and housing needs.

Susan Shaer is executive director of WAND, Women's Action for New Directions, a national organization that aims to reduce militarism and violence and redirect excessive military spending. She also leads WiLL, the Women Legislators' Lobby, and has helped elect 34 women who are currently members of Congress.

Eleanor Smeal is the publisher of Ms. magazine and the president of the Feminist Majority Foundation (www.feminist.org). She is a former two-term president of the National Organization for Women.

Hilda L. Solis, now in her second term in the House of Representatives, is the first Latina to serve on the House Energy and Commerce Committee. In 2000, she was awarded the John F. Kennedy Profile in Courage Award for her pioneering work on environmental justice issues in California. Her priorities are protecting the environment, improving the quality of health care, and fighting for the rights of working families.

Alison Stein is a founder and coordinator of the Younger Women's Task Force, and a program assistant at the National Council of Women's Organizations. She was a 2003–2004 fellow at the Institute for Women's Policy Research and has worked on women's issues in Tanzania and Ghana.

Stacey Stewart is president and CEO of the Fannie Mae Foundation (www. fanniemaefoundation.org), the nation's largest private nonprofit foundation devoted exclusively to affordable housing and the revitalization of communities. Stewart, a working mother, is widely recognized as a powerful advocate for women's financial independence, both in her professional capacity and in her private life.

C. DeLores Tucker, Ph.D., is the convening founder and the national chair of the National Congress of Black Women. An active participant in the civil rights movement throughout her life, Dr. Tucker was the only African American woman to serve as secretary of state in Pennsylvania.

Melanne Verveer chairs the Vital Voices Global Partnership (www.vitalvoices. org), an international nonprofit that supports emerging women leaders in building democracies and strong economies. In her long career, she has been assistant to the president of the United States, chief of staff for First Lady Hillary Clinton, and executive vice president of People For the American Way.

Frieda Werden has been active in alternative media since 1973. In 1985, she cofounded WINGS: Women's International News Gathering Service (www.wings.org). She currently serves on the boards of the International Association of Women in Radio and Television (www.iawrt.org) and Association Mondiale des Radios Diffuseurs Communautaires (www.amarc.org). In her home city of Vancouver, Canada, she works at CJSF-FM (www.cjsf.ca), the campus radio station of Simon Fraser University.

Marie Wilson is the president and founder of The White House Project (www. thewhitehouseproject.org). A longtime advocate of women's issues, she's also cocreator of Take Daughters to Work Day, author of *Closing the Leadership Gap*, and president emerita of the Ms. Foundation for Women, which she led for 20 years.

Pamela Wilson is the assistant to the president in the Department for Professional Employees at the AFL-CIO, a coalition of 25 unions representing four million professional, technical, and clerical workers. She has also worked for the building trades unions and the unions representing food and service workers.

Cathleen Witter is a project director for Turner Strategies, a public relations firm specializing in strategic communications for public policy issues. She has also served as director of policy and communications for a think tank specializing in women's health care, and she currently cochairs the Younger Women's Task Force for the National Council of Women's Organizations (www.womensorganizations.org).

Laura M. Young, Ph.D., is executive director of OWL, The Voice of Midlife and

Older Women, the only national grassroots membership organization to focus solely on issues unique to women as they age (www.owl-national.org). She has more than 25 years of experience coordinating treatment services for people with a variety of serious mental illnesses.

June Zeitlin is the executive director of WEDO (Women's Environment and Development Organization; www.wedo.org). Prior to this, she worked at the Ford Foundation, focusing on women's rights and opportunities. She has more than 25 years of experience as a lawyer and advocate for women's rights.

Diana Zuckerman, Ph.D., is president of the National Research Center for Women & Families (www.center4research.org), a research and advocacy organization. She is a nationally respected health and policy expert who has been on the faculty of Vassar College and Yale University, conducted research at Harvard University, and held senior policy positions in the U.S. Congress and the White House.

Elaine Zuckerman, founder and president of Gender Action, worked inside the World Bank from 1981 to 1990 and 1998 to 2000; while there, she created the first program to mitigate the harmful impacts of economic restructuring on the poor, especially women. She has also been coordinator of the Social Policy Agenda Group at the InterAmerican Development Bank.